9/83

D1261406

Truman
Capote

Truman Capote

The Story of His Bizarre and Exotic Boyhood
by an Aunt Who Helped Raise Him

MARIE RUDISILL

with

JAMES C. SIMMONS

William Morrow and Company, Inc. • *New York* • *1983*

Library of Congress Cataloging in Publication Data

Rudisill, Marie.
Truman Capote : the story of his bizarre and exotic
boyhood by an aunt who helped raise him.

Includes index.
1. Capote, Truman, 1924–   —Biography—Youth.
2. Authors, American—20th century—Biography.
I. Simmons, James C.   II. Title.
PS3505.A59Z87 1983   813'.54 [B]   82-18783
ISBN 0-688-01590-5

Printed in the United States of America

First Edition

1 2 3 4 5 6 7 8 9 10

BOOK DESIGN BY LINEY LI

For James E. Rudisill

ACKNOWLEDGMENTS

To Julian Bach, our agent,
for his untiring efforts and understanding.

A special thanks from Marie Rudisill
to Roberta Ashley of *Cosmopolitan*
for her encouragement and inspiration.

To Hillel Black, our editor,
and to Jane Meara, assistant editor,
for their wonderful cooperation.

Truman
Capote

*The words of his mouth were smoother than butter,
but war was in his heart; his words were softer than oil,
yet were they drawn swords.*

PSALMS 55:21

The Funeral:
January 5, 1954

THE FIFTH DAY OF JANUARY 1954 was freezing in New York, but you could never tell that by the way Truman Capote was dressed. The thermometer hovered in the mid-twenties while a cold wind as shrill as a calliope whipped through the city. But there was Truman. No hat. No gloves. No overcoat. All that stood between him and the cold was a black velvet suit he had just bought in Europe.

"Why hadn't she waited?" Truman wanted to know. "Why hadn't Mother waited just a few more days for me to get back from Italy? *Why?*"

Four days earlier, after a New Year's Eve of heavy drinking, aimless flirting, and a big blow-out with her husband, Joe, Truman's mother and my sister, Lillie Mae Faulk Persons Capote, had taken an overdose of sleeping pills in her luxurious apartment at 1060 Park Avenue and committed suicide. She was found the next morning, sprawled over the edge of the bed, arms dangling on the floor as though she had tried to reach for the telephone. Her night-table drawer was pulled out, and a bottle of sleeping pills had spilled into the drawer and onto the floor beside the bed. The funeral was scheduled for the fifth of January at 11:00 A.M.

As Truman and I walked down Madison Avenue toward Campbell's Funeral Home at 81st Street, my heart almost broke for him. This would be a tough day for all of us in the family, but it would be pure torture for Lillie Mae's only child, who was about to turn thirty.

Finally, Truman would have to come face to face with the inescapable truth—that he and his mother were never going to get that chance at a decent relationship. The last opportunity—halfhearted as it was—was now lost forever with the finality of her death.

Truman and his mother had never been close. Lillie Mae had summarily dropped Truman into our family circle in Monroeville, Alabama, whenever he stood in the way of her climb upward to the Social Register. Poor Truman grew up thinking that every child lived in a big house with three spinster cousins, three aunts, a bachelor cousin, and two female servants. He had always hidden his mother's true nature from himself. Now he had to come to terms with the whole ugly mess. Lillie Mae's timing had been lousy, no question of that.

Truman was riding the wave of literary acclaim. He had spent the previous month in D. H. Lawrence's house in Palermo, Sicily. He was, literally, on top of the world. Yet while an enthusiastic but anonymous public cheered his talent, his very own flesh-and-blood mother didn't think he was worth even saying good-bye to.

The funeral guests had started arriving an hour before Truman and I walked into Campbell's—what few guests there were. Lillie Mae and her second husband, Joe Capote, had what you might call occasional friends in New York's fast-spending café society. Few of them decided to attend the service. Betty Sinclair, the oil heiress, for example, didn't bother to come around. Nor did Gloria Stump of the Stump and Walters Seed Company. Or Hans Yaeger, the big shot from American Cyanamid.

Not only did most of her friends pull a no-show, but so did many of Lillie Mae's very own relatives. My cousin Jenny—the family matriarch whose word was family law and whose incredible industry and enterprise had saved our family from ruin and poverty—had been turned down in her request to have the funeral moved south. In retaliation she had refused to come to New York for the service. Lord knows how many more people would have shown up if Jenny had come north.

Among the roses, the lilies of the valley, the lavender orchids, and the purple violets, Lillie Mae lay in pale blue chiffon. Even in death in her silver-handled casket, she was a beautiful woman. And even in death she was a problem child. Lillie Mae had left instructions that she was to be cremated, a family first (another first had been her divorce) and another reason Jenny didn't feel compelled to attend the funeral.

As I looked at Lillie Mae resting serenely in her expensive coffin, I remembered how her drinking had made my life so miserable. Toward the end of her life she usually called me three or four times a week to complain about God and her son Truman, both of whom had disappointed her terribly. She had often talked about death that last year, sometimes as a release and other times as a horror. I thought, too, how completely she had dominated our childhood world, remembering that now with a sad, sick jealousy.

The fifteen or so "mourners" acted more like guests at a cocktail party, wandering around, showing off expensive mourning dresses, and chatting about everything except poor Lillie Mae.

The Alabama relatives, the handful who did come north, were a bit more somber, of course, dressed in their finest Sabbath array. They may have appeared shabby and unstylish by the standards of New York, especially the women with their hats trimmed with faded artificial flowers. But they all thought of themselves as the last of the true Southern aristocrats. (Truman has always played down the family's money in his writings and interviews.)

From Monroeville, Alabama—where Lillie Mae had deposited Truman so many times and which served as the setting for some of his best-known works, such as *A Christmas Memory* and *The Grass Harp*—had come Uncle Howard and his wife, Abeygale; my sisters Lucille and Mary Ida; and Nelle Harper Lee, who had grown up next door to us.

Every Southern family has its Uncle Howards and Aunt Abeygales. Howard was an incorrigible drunkard and mean as hell to boot. He kept a high-yellow mistress, Nevada, with four or five off-color yard children in Rooktown, the Negro shanty-town outside Monroeville. After a night out with Nevada, Howard would lie in bed until he heard Abbie in the kitchen and smelled the aroma of fresh coffee. Then he would come into the kitchen, sneak up behind Abbie, and clamp his dirty, fat fingers over her nose. "Do you smell that, woman?" he would demand, his breath still reeking of moonshine. "Now *that* is the smell of *real* pussy!"

Abeygale was a thin-faced, waspish woman with thick-rimmed glasses so large they made her look like a lemur. Her chest was flat and hardly marked by the faintest peaks of breasts. She was tall, thin, and ungainly, with large feet and rawboned hands. She wore her hair, thin and greasy black streaked with gray, pulled back tightly into a bun. One look at her and you knew why her husband had shopped for his pleasures in Rooktown.

"My God! Truman's mother a suicide!" Uncle Howard whispered in shocked disbelief.

"Well, I always said that Lillie Mae was much too beautiful for her own good," Abeygale insisted, spiteful to the end.

Lucille, Lillie Mae's and my younger sister, had a pretty, serene face highlighted by large brown eyes. When she was still an infant, she had developed a severe infection in both her ears that made her completely deaf by the age of three. Lucille appears in several of Truman's stories and in his first novel, *Other Voices, Other Rooms*. In that book he describes Joel, the narrator, doing "hateful things such as tease his older cousin, a dumb-looking girl named Louise, because she was a little deaf. He'd cup his ear and cry, 'Aye, aye' and couldn't stop until she broke into tears." Truman did just that to Lucille when he was a youngster. (He has always had a bad habit of making fun of others' physical impairments.) Lucille was obviously not a favorite with her nephew; Truman repeatedly thwarted her attempts to hug him at the funeral.

Truman had always been fonder of our other sister Mary Ida, a strong, unyielding, and self-reliant woman. She always was a soft touch for animals. One day Mary Ida found a buzzard nearly dead from an injury, nursed it back to health, and even taught it how to fly again. Mary Ida, as it turned out, was a softer touch for buzzards than for people. She refused to allow Nelle Harper Lee—who had been Truman's closest friend as a child and would go on to win a Pulitzer Prize for her novel *To Kill a Mockingbird*—to ride in our family car to the crematorium, stating emphatically that it was for "family only." Truman protested and then finally gave in to her wishes. He was always weak that way.

Although those relatives who refused to make the trip to New York could forget Lillie Mae, no man who had ever loved my sister could. Proof of that was in the funeral parlor that day. All three of her lovers had signed the register. Each was as different from the others as apples from peaches and plums.

The first man in Lillie Mae's life was the most exotic. He was a Creek Indian named Tecumseh, whom we always called Teshu. Tall, graceful, and still sexy even then in his paunchless middle age, Tecumseh was the proud great-grandson of Chief Red Eagle, who had been a plantation owner on the banks of the Alabama River in Clairborne, a few miles from Monroeville. (It is a curious historical fact, but in our part of the Old South many of the Indians kept slaves themselves.) Tecumseh and Lillie Mae were passionately in love, but my sister's cowardly refusal to step forth in society on the arm of an Indian doomed the affair and eventually split them up. Tecumseh for the rest of his life could never bring himself to love another woman.

Archulus Persons, Jr., Lillie Mae's first husband and Truman's father, stood somewhat apart from the other mourners. He was a tall, thin man with thick-lensed glasses and cold eyes. Arch Persons had come to Lillie Mae with an impressive pedigree. His family was socially prominent, wealthy, and dedicated to public service. His father had been a famous professor of chemistry at the University of Alabama; President Theodore Roosevelt had once invited him to Washington to consult on some matter. His uncle was a prominent doctor in Montgomery with degrees from a Viennese medical school. His brothers were successful businessmen, and his sisters had married well.

Arch had a law degree from Washington and Lee University in Lexington, Virginia, but Arch never practiced law; he used it. He was a promoter, flamboyant in his expensive silk suits and wide-brimmed panama hats. We all thought of him as a reincarnation of P. T. Barnum. (Truman probably picked up his own sense of showmanship from his father.)

After Arch and Lillie Mae married, they traveled all over the South together, hustling various enterprises from their headquarters in New Orleans. They promoted some weird things over the years. One time, for example, Arch found himself an Egyptian fellow named Hadjah who knew how to control his breathing. The gimmick was that Arch would sell tickets to people who wanted to see Hadjah buried alive in a coffin in the ground. The act worked pretty well and made them all lots of money.

Eventually, the novelty of Arch Persons's bizarre business schemes wore off. Lillie Mae won an Elizabeth Arden beauty contest (but never the title of Miss Alabama, as Truman keeps insisting on those talk shows) and got a free trip to New York as first prize. There she met the third man in her life, the chubby little Cuban gentleman, Joe Capote, who stood in the corner for almost the entire funeral service and rarely spoke to anyone.

Lillie Mae managed a restaurant called the Green Line in the Wall Street area. One day Capote, a controller at a big textile firm, walked in. Lillie Mae turned to a waitress and said, "That's the man I'm going to marry!" Never mind that at the time she was *already* married. As far as she was concerned, it was all over with Arch, only he didn't know it.

Joe Capote set Lillie Mae up in a fancy apartment on Riverside Drive. To her credit, she did take Truman out of our house in Monroeville and bring him to New York. It was a mistake to enroll him in a military school, as they did, but it was good that Lillie Mae at last began to understand that she had to care for her ten-year-old son.

My husband, Jim, spent more time with Joe than I did. Joe was a big horse player, sometimes dropping two grand on a single race. Jim often went along for the ride. Joe was always working on shady business deals that were just inside the law. Finally, one of those deals crossed that boundary because he eventually ended up in Sing Sing for embezzlement. But until then he spent money as if it were water, and Joe and Lillie Mae lived a flashy life in New York. Truman probably put some of Joe Capote into his character of Jose Ybarra-Jaeger, Holly's rich Brazilian playboy suitor in *Breakfast at Tiffany's.*

For Joe the pain of Lillie Mae's death was less than he had thought it would be, and the joy of reunion with her son Truman was less than he had hoped. His manner at the funeral was repressed and watchful.

(This is probably as good a place as any to clear up, once and for all, the confusion over Truman's name. His complete name is Truman Streckfus Persons Capote. His first name comes from Arch's friend Truman More, a businessman from Denver, Colorado. Vern Streckfus owned a steamship line in New Orleans where Arch worked for a long time; Truman once tap-danced for Louis Armstrong, who played the trumpet on board one of Streckfus's ships. Persons is, of course, Arch's last name; Capote is Joe's.)

Arch always resented the fact that Truman, when he grew up, took the name of Capote instead of Persons. Never one to beat around the bush, he confronted Truman at the funeral.

"You loved your mother, didn't you, Truman?" he asked, turning the knife.

Truman bristled. What right did his father have to cross-examine him now? He answered quickly, "Did you love her?"

Arch tried again. "Why in God's name did your mother insist on being cremated?"

Truman answered slowly. "Because she had a fear of the grave, of the darkness, and the earth."

Exasperated by the line of questioning, Truman turned to me. "Tiny," he said (this has always been the family's nickname for me), "let's slip out for a drink. I need to talk to you and get away from this loathsome place."

We managed to escape through the lobby of Campbell's Funeral Home into the cold, brisk air. We walked down Madison Avenue and crossed over to Longchamps. It no longer exists, but in those days Longchamps was an elite place to eat. At the time Truman's tastes ran toward the garish, and Longchamps with its circus bar certainly filled the bill.

The restaurant was practically full with a late luncheon crowd and early-afternoon drinkers. The headwaiter led us to a table in the rear. Several people recognized my nephew. One young girl approached our table with a menu and pencil in hand and requested his autograph. Truman, however, turned and waved her away without saying a word. Our waiter came over immediately and Truman ordered. "Two Beefeater's with Schweppes. In perfectly plain glasses."

This was another of Truman's quirks, like walking around

in midwinter without an overcoat. He insisted on never drinking anything out of a glass that was not perfectly plain crystal. In fact, one night he had even refused a drink at my house because the glass had a simple gold border.

"Tiny, darling," Truman said, "I have not had a bite to eat all day. I think I know your taste in food; at least I *should* after all these years. Shall I order for both of us?"

Truman beckoned to the waiter and in complete disregard of the menu ordered. "We will have two of the same—curry of shrimp, light on the curry, saffron rice, tossed green salad with bleu-cheese dressing, coffee later, no dessert."

Truman was right. He knew my taste in food.

We sat there quietly for a few moments until Truman finally brought up the subject of his mother.

"It was just last month before I left for Italy," he said, "that Mother and I had a very close talk. It was the first time we were in complete understanding. We had never talked so freely before. Maybe it's because she recognized my fame in international social circles. My contacts with Grace Kelly and Princess Margaret were *so* important to her. Whatever the reason, I felt that she was finally accepting me as I am, and to me that was a great victory. You know, my way of life was always her most bitter disappointment. She wanted me to be another Jack Dempsey."

I was way past shock on this subject, of course, but I was still stubborn. At one time I, too, had figured that Truman was just going through a phase. My only worry was that someone was going to hurt him, beat him up. I wanted him to have at least the trappings of a normal life.

"You know," I said to him, "you can't buck and defy society, Truman."

"I want my place in society—mine, not theirs."

I shrugged. "Is that what you really want?"

"I only know what I feel, and following the feeling is only the beginning. I realize this. It will be enough for a while."

"Truman, have you ever thought of marriage?"

"Yes, at one time I did. I thought of the permanence of marriage and perhaps having a child, the joy of that. But I detest men who marry and have their little affairs on the side. Their wives are tense, edgy things instead of women in full bloom, so to speak. And there is another thing, Tiny. The marriage of a virile woman and an effeminate man only causes the strength of one to be sucked out by the other. It is not worth it."

I felt as cold as the ice in my empty glass. But I brought myself to say it. "I had always hoped that you and Nelle . . ."

As soon as I said "Nelle," I realized I had gone too far. A silence, like a black-winged bird, suddenly descended over the table, and it made me stop talking.

Truman has always had a little dramatic habit he drops into whenever he's confronted with a difficult question. He takes a long time to answer and usually fiddles with something in his hand. As a child he would turn his ice-cream cone around in his hand and lick it on all sides until it was even. He was doing this now but with the drink in his hand instead of an ice-cream cone. He turned the glass around and around and examined it from every angle before finally speaking, very softly and in a deeper voice than usual.

"Tiny, why should I probe and dissect my emotions? I want to be a great writer. If it means playing a big game to have my own way, well, I will. I will move *all* the pawns."

He turned to me and, for a moment, his face seemed to melt. It startled me, but in another second his face was normal. Long-ago events came back to life as we talked and ate. Truman touched lightly on weighty matters, and I knew he had more to tell me.

He continued. "Tiny, I began going to bed with men very

early. Without fear and without shame. I felt whole and healthy for the first time. I made them happy, and I made myself happy."

This kind of talk made me afraid for him—afraid that he would be physically hurt. Even as a kid I had stuck up for Truman whenever one of the more he-man relatives would start to smirk at him. I could never stand that. I was afraid, too, that the emotional penalties of a homosexual life would bear heavily on a gifted person like Truman. He has always had a softness in him, a sort of dependency. I was afraid to let him go. I could fight off his attackers, but could he? We go way back on this. Once when he was sixteen, as we sat on the back porch in Monroeville, he told me in his own words, "I will be a brilliant, delicate, sissy, queer, homo—or shall I be formal, darling, and say 'homosexual'?"

The books tell us there are many forks in the road leading to homosexuality. But when Truman's mother was first confronted with the fact that her son was "different," she was utterly revolted. She knew I thought her attitude was heinous, and it was a closed subject between us. If I had talked with her about this, I always feared I would lose control of myself and bring up all sorts of other gripes I had about her methods of child rearing. Unfortunately, her reaction to Truman's sexual inclinations caused him to retreat into a smaller and smaller circle. He was like a toad in a hole. But then, after he had quietly accepted the facts about himself, he told me it was like looking beyond an open door and catching a glimpse of clear starry sky just beginning to lighten in the morning.

"Our lives," he continued, "are meant to be nothing but a series of love affairs . . . nothing more. Drink up."

Truman has always said, even back in Monroeville, that *love* is the most hopeful word in any language. But I began to wonder if it would be enough. He shared one of my fears.

"Tiny, it's not how I will live that terrifies me. It is what the extension of time will do to my life when the gratifications of the young may no longer be possible. Before I left for Europe, Mother insisted that I see an analyst. He advised me to get less neurotic hobbies than fornication and booze. 'Do you know of any other options?' he asked me. 'Yes,' I told him. 'Murder.' He laughed. But the poor man—if he only knew of the agonizing and perfect end that I had concocted for him!"

"Truman," I said, trying one more time, "I don't believe that self-gratification is the true purpose in life. You cannot let sex dominate your life to this extent."

"I tell you, Tiny," the gentle voice continued, "this matter should be left to the individual conscience. It would be better for everyone to decide the ethics of the question of sex for himself or herself."

"I know, Truman, that you have been given a rare and beautiful talent. Develop it, use it. Be careful of your personal life, or you will wake up and realize one morning that your doll is stuffed with sawdust."

"Darling Tiny, I know you think I am exceptional and have great potential. I believe I have, too. I don't know—perhaps it is instinct—but I know I can write. I do not underestimate my ability. I love you for believing in me."

We finished our coffee and brandy. It was time to get back to his mother's apartment. Members of the family would be expecting us.

"God," Truman said, "I can't bear to go back to all that crying and kissing."

"And that's not the worst part of it," I reminded him. No, the worst part would be all those veiled references to his mother's suicide, all that whispering, all those relatives hovering about with their gratuitous advice.

"Truman," I finally asked, right before we were ready to leave, "do you really think that Lillie Mae meant to kill herself?"

It was a very painful thing to ask and maybe even a little

cruel. Truman carefully inspected the nails on each of his hands—those damned theatrics again—and then straightened his glasses. Finally, he answered.

"Yes, I do. She had her reasons, but the one thing I am grateful for is that at least *I* was not the reason. When she called me in Europe and told me about the trouble Joe Capote was having with his firm over the fraud suit, I should have come home immediately. She explained that Joe had lost his job and would be prosecuted for the embezzlement of company funds. My mother just couldn't accept the fact that all of a sudden she had no money. The final blow came the day that Joe pawned her full-length mink coat." (Joe Capote was later found guilty of fraud in excess of $125,000 and in 1955 was sent to Sing Sing to serve a three-year term.)

"Truman," I said. "I know you tried to make some kind of restitution but it was rejected." (He really could not raise the money, much as he wanted to.)

We put our arms around each other and walked from the restaurant. It was a long walk to the apartment at 1060 Park Avenue. The sky was sloppy. A brisk wind whipped trash along the gutters and caused passersby to clutch their hats. Mounds of dirty snow edged the cold, hard sidewalks. Shards of ice filled the slush holes in the streets.

As we trudged along, our minds seemed to turn to brighter and happier times, perhaps as an escape for both of us.

"Truman, eating that curry of shrimp in the restaurant reminded me of the time you and writer Donald Windham visited us in Charlotte, North Carolina. I had a large buffet dinner for you and served curry of shrimp in a silver chafing dish. You announced to the whole party, 'I have eaten all over the world, but this is the best curry of shrimp I have ever tasted.' Later on I remember seeing you standing by the chafing dish with a big serving spoon just shoveling the shrimp down without even bothering about a plate. One prominent Charlotte attorney approached you and invited you to lunch with him at an exclusive Charlotte country club. Do you remember what you said to him?"

"Sure do. I told him to go shit on a stick."

"Whatever possessed you to say a thing like that?"

"Simply because he was a nobody, and he only wanted to be seen with a somebody."

"Why are you smiling, Truman?"

"I didn't know I was. Maybe it's because we are enjoying ourselves."

When we finally reached our destination at 86th and Park, we took the service elevator so that nobody would see us enter Joe and Lillie Mae's apartment. As we let ourselves in, Truman said, "Let's go to the maid's room and talk some more."

We found a half-full bottle of J & B Scotch on the kitchen table and took it with us.

"Truman, does Monroeville, Alabama, seem far away?" I asked him after we had settled into chairs and poured ourselves drinks.

"No," he answered. "Monroeville is bound up with my childhood more than any other thing. It has a queer power over me and the way I write and think."

"Well, Truman," I said, "Monroeville was the center, the positive and concrete center, for *all* our lives."

"Tiny," he said, "being back in America and being with you, even though my mother is dead, has made this day one I want to hold in my hand to peek at frequently, the way a child carries a nickel around in his tight fist, comforted in just knowing it's there."

"You're wrong, Truman, you are so very wrong," I told him. "The house is still there. Just as. it was when you lived there. In fact, *everything* you need is there."

That's when Truman started to cry. He cried as a small boy cries, pressing his mouth hard against the white knuckles of his fist.

CHAPTER ONE

Jenny's House

MONROEVILLE, ALABAMA, where Truman spent his first seven years, is a crossroads town in the Deep South, midway between Montgomery and Mobile. Sixty years ago it was pretty much the same as a hundred other such towns in the South. The architecture of its business section was undistinguished, all the buildings being either ugly brick or sun-bleached wood with their awnings, once garishly striped, now weather-beaten and torn.

A courthouse with a pyramid-shaped roof and clock-studded tower dominated the center of the square. Chiseled into plain white marble above the entrance were the words "MONROE COUNTY COURTHOUSE, MONROEVILLE, ALABAMA." (The interior was used in the filming of *To Kill a Mockingbird*.) The sidewalks around the square were paved, but the streets were Alabama clay, which turned into a red mushy mire during the winter rains and restless dust during the summer droughts.

Throughout the warmer months the old men congregated on benches on the courthouse grass, playing checkers, chewing tobacco, whittling sticks, or simply passing time, their liver-spotted hands crooked on their hickory sticks. It was the sort of place the local undertaker looked at with confidence, knowing that he was never going to starve as long as there was that much work cut out for him.

Old man Junious Odom was the official commentator of the group. He had a meager fringe of white hair around the base of his skull, which was otherwise completely bald and shone like old ivory. The sharp, bony structure of his face showed through his yellowish skin. "Lord," he would say, "take a look at Miss Tru Ella. I'll be doggone if her backside don't put me in mind of a battleship down in Mobile Bay. It's big enough to smother a man." Then the others would join in with sly winks and toothless laughter.

On one side of the square was Dr. Fripp's general store, a most heavenly place for children. He stocked candy, toys, crepe paper, and party favors, in addition to kitchen appliances, tools, and other miscellaneous merchandise. Inside you could hear: "Dr. Fripp, I'se would like a pair o' dem pink bloomers, please, sir."

"What size?"

"I'se railly does not know 'cause I ain't never bot ary pair till now."

"Well, what in tarnation do you want them for now?"

"'Cause, Dr. Fripp, de flies an' de gnats is so bad."

And Dr. Fripp's face would turn red as a poppy.

On another side of the square was the town drugstore. An old metal sign flapped in the breeze out front, its gilt background long since peeled away, the name, MONROE DRUGS, almost faded into obscurity. The interior was taken up with ancient wire-legged tables surrounded by rickety chairs and a marvelous white marble counter that boasted a row of high stools in front and a streaked mirror behind. There you went to get your prescription filled by Mr. Yarborough, the druggist, provided you did not come in between noon and one o'clock because that was lunchtime. Kids on their way home from school, toting shoulder bags, sometimes filled with books, sometimes with stiff dead cats, always stopped by the drugstore to order a lemon Coke, a cherry pop, or banana split.

Monroeville's heart was the square, with the rest of our town radiating beyond. Many of the houses were large and encrusted in the opulent gingerbread Gothic that had been the popular architectual style for so many years. The streets were lined with great oaks, heavy with curtains of matted moss that swung softly in the evening breezes. There were three churches—the Baptist, the Methodist, and the Mount Zion, the last for the Negroes. (Our family belonged to the Baptist.)

This was an earlier America of ladies' sewing circles and garden clubs, church socials, a solitary picture show that exhibited movies only on Friday and Saturday (silent, of course, with a piano accompaniment), of weddings with old shoes and white ribbons, and county fairs with blue ribbons for the best cakes and pies. As in so many Southern towns in the early part of this century, people in Monroeville were born, lived, and died without ever once thinking seriously about moving away. The descendants of the original families, who had settled the wilderness when Indians roamed the forests, farmed their lands, ran their businesses, and married into other families just as old, sometimes too close to their bloodlines.

Truman's happiest years as a youth were spent in this town. Jenny, Callie, Sook, and Bud Faulk were the distant cousins with whom Truman shared his childhood. None had ever taken a mate. They all lived together under Jenny's firm hand in a huge, rambling white frame house, very near the square, that was cool and delightful in summer but too drafty and cold in the winter. It was the kind of home that gathers memories like dust, a place filled with laughter and joy, pain and heartbreak.

To us children (for Jenny's house had been home to me, too, along with Truman's mother, Lillie Mae), the entrance hall appeared as large as the average small house. The ceilings seemed to reach to the beyond. About halfway down the hall, Jenny had built bookcases on either side, flanked by two round pillars that rose with great majesty to the ceiling. Whenever I entered the house, those towering pillars always caught my eyes, pulling them upward to the ornate scrollwork on top.

The dining room represented Jenny and her life of careful acquisition. The furniture, even the silver and china, had been the same for at least thirty years. Along one wall a serpentine-front china cabinet overflowed with Dresden, Meissen, and sparkling pieces of cut glass. Jenny would tap a piece of glass with her fingernail, making a bell-like sound, or pick up a piece of Meissen and say, "This belonged to Aunt Fronie." Her pride was a Lannuier dining-room table with an Anthony Quervelle sideboard. The set was large and heavy in appearance but imposing. It suited Jenny perfectly. She loved her antiques, and yet she never regarded them as museum pieces. Never did she reprimand a child for touching any of her prizes. I recall one occasion when she allowed the young Truman to shake the prisms on the enormous basket chandelier to set them dancing and tinkling.

A wide veranda went around the front of the house and disappeared in the back. The backyard was both a delight and a frustration. Trellis upon trellis held twisted, tortured wisteria vines, which hung like an ominous blue curtain, blotting out our view of the town. The yard was filled to overflowing with japonicas, azaleas, and walls of blue hydrangeas. Somehow each spring the King Alfred daffodils managed to rear their heads and bloom. There was no order or rhythm to the garden.

Surrounding this landscaper's nightmare was a tall fence made of animal bones. Jenny had ordered them hauled to Monroeville from an animal graveyard in Clairborne, Alabama, and then supervised the selection and laying of each bone as the fence slowly took shape. "No," she would say firmly, "the backbone can't be next to the foot bone; that isn't right. You have to fit the backbone to the hipbone." And so the gruesome fence had finally been completed after many months of hawk-eyed supervision. I remember hearing it told how one worker had bumped his wheelbarrow into the fence, causing an avalanche of bones to come crashing down. Thereupon, Jenny gave him such a tongue-lashing that he took off like a scared jackrabbit and never returned. To Jenny, the fence was a triumphant achievement, a monumental tribute to things dead, living, and yet to come. The house has since burned down (to be rebuilt on the same foundations), but Jenny's bone fence still stands, grimly defying fire and the elements.

Jenny was a beautiful woman, even in her fifties. She had frosty blue eyes, red hair, and skin like a china doll's. She was on the short side, but her sharp tongue gave her added stature. Her temper was as swift and sure as the striking head of a snake. She was always a woman to be reckoned with.

I don't wish to give the impression that Jenny was a bitter and hardened woman, lacking in kindness and gentleness. This was not so. She had as many facets to her character as the crystal prisms in her chandelier. Each new twist of circumstances brought forth its complementary emotion. She expressed without inhibition all her feelings, whether they were gentle, cruel, or cowardly.

Jenny was born Virginia Herd Faulk on July 19, 1873, the third child to William Jasper and Samantha Elizabeth Faulk. Her arrival coincided with the Crash of 1873 which caught the nation unawares. Panic spread across the country, and the stock exchanges closed for the first time in history. This was eight years after Lee surrendered to Grant at Appomattox.

The Faulks lived on a piney-woods plantation, known as Faulk's Plantation, located eight miles from Monroeville. William Faulk had inherited the land (about 2,000 acres), but he built the plantation with his own sweat and toil. By the outbreak of the Civil War on April 12, 1861, he had established himself as one of the largest slave owners and cotton growers in our section of Alabama. Jenny used to insist he had owned upward of 150 slaves.

There seems to have been little doubt that William and Samantha had created for themselves a grand life-style in those years just before the war. They had built a large plantation house in the typical Georgian style of the period. It had two stories with white columns and a wide veranda in the front. A broad hallway started at the oversized front door and ran the length of the house to the rear. When they gave a ball, the hall was where they had the dancing. There were two parlors, one for everyday matters and the other a sitting room for more formal occasions. In the rear were a dining room, a library, and a downstairs bedroom. The kitchen was completely detached from the main house, as was typical of the buildings of the day. The walkway between the two buildings was enclosed, so that the servants could bring the food to the dining room without chilling it.

In the back was a spring house sunk into the ground and built out of solid rock. It survived long after the big plantation house had been reduced to weed-covered foundations and four rotting columns. Originally, the spring house had two divisions, one side being for butter, eggs, and milk; the other for cider, vegetables, and fruits. Water from an underground artesian spring trickled constantly down the walls, so that it was damp and cool always, even in the hottest summer weather.

William enlisted in the calvary in the early months of the Civil War and was soon made an officer. He saw combat in some of the bloodiest campaigns, including Shiloh and Chickamauga. For years his sword hung in its original scabbard over the fireplace in Bud's bedroom. It was destroyed when the house burned in 1952.

Finally the war came to an end, and the South lost everything it cherished. The whole region mourned its dead, its deep hurt. Many Southerners had lost their citizenship, homes, and possessions. They became psychological aliens in their own land. Suddenly, four million Negroes were freed with nowhere to go, nowhere to sleep, no work, no food, no schools, no "place." The hated Yankee accent was everywhere, as thousands of dreaded carpetbaggers poured into the South. For a time the chaos of peace replaced the chaos of war.

Southwestern Alabama had been spared the horrors of Sherman's march to the sea, but its people were still in a state of shock. Many in Mobile had been impoverished overnight with the collapse of the Confederate currency. Hundreds of widows and orphans there had to the end held nearly all their assets in Confederate dollars. General Dabney Maury, the Confederate general in charge of the Gulf, had assured them that he could hold Mobile against a six months' siege from the whole army and navy of the United States. Almost to the last day their confidence remained unshaken. The surrender came without a word of warning.

The Alabamians in Mobile and the adjacent countryside to the north and west had not yet recovered from the shock of the surrender when William returned to his plantation. Few people then had definite plans for the future. Some thought of going to Brazil. Others hoped to get away from the "sassy free niggers" by going north. Scarcely any regarded their chance of cultivating their lands with free Negro labor as hopeful. Most were troubled by a vague, uncertain fear that in one way or another they would lose their lands.

William assessed his own very considerable personal losses. The slave quarters out back stood empty, gaunt, and silent, their whitewash peeling off like leprous skin, the former slaves scattered to the far corners of the county. (In the 1850s a prime field hand had sold for around $1,600.) His lovely plantation house was in shambles. The exquisitely carved Adam mantels and the heavily embossed brass doorknobs had been sold or stolen. Drapes of luminous brocade hung in tatters over the windows. The spokes from his fine carriage had been chopped into kindling. The brick walkway was chipped and broken.

At first William tried to recoup his losses by planting cotton on a portion of his 2,000 acres. But most of his former slaves had moved away. He and Samantha started to raise a family, perhaps as an expression of optimism that things had to get better. Bud, the first, came along on March 16, 1869; Sook on June 16, 1871; Jenny on July 19, 1873; and finally Callie on March 10, 1875. They were all children of a lost war who grew up with the knowledge of what life can be like in a defeated country, when lived on the bare bones of privation.

By the time of the birth of his last child, William had simply given up. Without the help of slaves he could not cope with the land, and he could never accept the fact that the gracious, slowly paced life of the Old South was gone forever. He lived over and over in his mind the glory of the Confederacy's lost cause. His force, energy, and spirit utterly exhausted, William was a mere shell of his former self. Finally he retired altogether from the management of his plantation and spent the rest of his life a pathetic eccentric, rocking away on his front porch, cursing the damned Yankees. He was little more than a ghost at the time of his death in 1899.

Samantha in her turn tried desperately to keep body and soul together. The war and the subsequent deprivations had completely stripped away her pride. She knew she could no longer raise a family in the leisurely and luxurious way of the Old South. Times had changed. Samantha brought her children through a period when even the most common staples were often in short supply. When she could not afford tea or coffee, she made do with burned corn and sassafras as substitutes. In the early years of Reconstruction she was actually afraid that the freed slaves who remained would rise up and murder her family.

But Samantha hid her fears. She went to work in the fields, supervising the handful of Negroes who agreed to work for wages. She planted cotton because that was all she knew—and all the whole South knew. As James Hammond had thundered from the floor of the U. S. Senate in the 1850s, "Cotton is king!" But in 1878, when Jenny was five years old, cotton sold for eight cents a pound, and it did not go up to eleven cents a pound until 1905.

Cotton. For some in the South it meant salvation; for many more it was a curse. In the 1870s and 1880s Samantha and her children worked the fields alongside the handful of former slaves who remained in the vicinity. They plowed the rich black bottomland into what a northern farmer would have called sweet-potato ridges. On the tops of those ridges, in separate hills, grew the soft and still tender cotton stalks that would blossom forth into red and white flowers. Even the cotton wore the Rebel colors! The petals were soft and flabby, and the flower was like a miniature hollyhock. For these "earliest blooms" Samantha and her children, like the other planters in the neighborhood, kept an eager watch, for to have the first was a prized distinction.

September was cotton-picking time. The hot sun of August would have burst the hard bolls open, and the fields about the Faulk Plantation would be white with the puffy fibers as far as the eye could see. It was a time of rejoicing for Samantha and her children, for the cotton—picked, ginned, and baled—meant a time of repayment of their debts to the local stores and the purchase of such luxuries as white flour (instead of cornmeal), sugar (instead of sorghum molasses), and perhaps some bolts of cloth to make new clothes. (To give you an idea of how bad things were in the South then, in 1880 the per capita wealth in the South was $376, compared to $1,186 for the rest of the country.)

But the harvest season was also a time of back-breaking labor on the Faulk Plantation. It meant hitting the floor even before dawn at the first crowing of the roosters, a hasty breakfast, and then a quick walk to the fields. Everyone did his or her share. No one was exempt. Samantha and her children worked side by side with their Negroes, the homemade cotton sacks hanging over their shoulders like crooked cowls.

By the time she was in her teens, Jenny was the overseer. This was not her choice; rather, no one else had the tenacity and courage to handle the field hands and the family members with anything like her firmness.

I was brought up on the story of Jenny's revolt against King Cotton. When she told it in later life, she would always start off by exclaiming, "I'd work my tailbone raw!" And then her anger, still fresh after all those years, would erupt. "Damn that cotton! Damn, damn that cotton!" she would cry.

Jenny told us often of the powerful stench of the horse dung and the outdoor privies on Faulk's Plantation, and the blowflies that were always present in great clouds during the warmer months. "I vow," she would say, "it was like being a first cousin to a hog."

Jenny always knew that she had to pick a hundred pounds of cotton a day or the others would be content with picking fifty pounds or less. When she had filled her cotton sack for the tenth time, she knew she would be over the one hundred mark. As the day progressed, the whole field became one sweat-blurred agony. Their bodies would ache from head to foot. The sticky heat and blinding sun only added to their burdens. Their belly muscles begged for mercy from carrying the heavy cotton sacks.

Bud recalled that in the fall of 1890 after the last boll of cotton had been picked clean, Jenny stumbled to a pine tree stump at the edge of the field, dropped her sack wearily to the ground, and sat down, utterly exhausted in body and spirit. She looked down at her dirty feet, her crusty brown legs, the blistered hands, and the knotty muscled arms. She picked up a piece of cotton from her bag and held it in her fingertips, studying it closely. Then she shouted, "Damn this cotton! The South is cursed! Every soul that it has ever suckled, white or niggers, has carried the curse of cotton!"

Suddenly, Jenny had had enough. She had lived with ugliness and poverty all her life. With drawers made out of "Lilly White Flour" bags. With flies, dirt, dung, and long days of exhausting work. She decided then and there—"*No more cotton!*"

Jenny was seventeen years old. She knew that she would have to pull away before another planting season started. Her one talent lay in sewing, so she decided to make a career out of designing and making women's hats. This appealed to her. Jenny took some money the family had saved and opened a tiny shop in the rear of a dry-goods store in Monroeville. Each day she walked the eight miles to town to tend her little shop and make her hats. Her business slowly grew.

Then a salesman from the Ely & Walker Mercantile Company in St. Louis saw some of her creations, which were selling as far away as Montgomery. He took several back to St. Louis and showed them to Mr. Ely. Soon afterward Jenny received an official invitation from Mr. Ely to come to St. Louis for formal training as a hat designer. He stipulated only that she remain in the city afterward to work with Ely & Walker. Jenny wrote Mr. Ely to say that she was grateful for the invitation and flattered by his recognition. She would accept his offer of training but would rather repay him later out of her earnings than continue on in St. Louis. She explained that she had to return to Monroeville to take care of her family. Mr. Ely was so impressed with one so young and talented that he agreed to help her.

Jenny went to St. Louis and studied under the designers at the Ely & Walker Company for six months. She returned to Monroeville with considerably more polish and sophistication than before. She reopened her hat business, renting a small one-room frame house for $3 a month.

This was the era of high-buttoned shoes, pearl-handled buttonhooks, and feather fans with multicolored tips fluttering beneath coquettish eyes. Poke bonnets were beginning to come into style. Almost anything of quality was "tailor made." Jenny quickly enlarged her business to include a selection of women's accessories.

Soon word got around about Jenny's hats. She had a great talent as a hat designer, no doubt of that. Women came from as far away as Birmingham, Montgomery, and Mobile to buy her custom-made hats. She made hats for weddings and all sorts of special occasions, fancy hats with ostrich plumes. Jenny went all out, and her customers loved it. Eventually she became so well known that buyers from the modish shops in New Orleans traveled to Monroeville to place their orders.

Her business prospered. But Jenny knew that she needed more capital for expansion. Otherwise, hers would continue to be a small-town operation in a one-room frame house, and she was much too ambitious to be content with such cramped quarters. Jenny wanted her own store on the square and a big house nearby in the fashionable part of town.

Her opportunity came in 1899 when her father died. Jenny took all the fine furniture (with the exception of a few Quervelle pieces), the sterling silver, the Pennsylvania dower chest that had belonged to Samantha's mother, quilts that had been in the family for over a century—anything that was worth a dollar—and sold them. A Mr. Albert Godchaux, an antiques and *objets d'art* dealer from New Orleans, came to the Faulk Plantation and bought the whole lot. Jenny struck a hard bargain and charmed him into paying a handsome sum.

In order to get control of the money from the sale of the household effects, Jenny made a solemn promise to Samantha, Callie, Sook, and Bud to provide for them as long as they lived if they gave her the use of the money without any interference. Jenny once told me that at the time she never thought they would take her up on her offer. But they did.

Jenny next purchased two lots in town, one for the store she wanted to build and another for her house. Jenny built her store on the square to the right of the courthouse. It was constructed out of red brick and occupied about one-third of the block. She supervised its construction with the same hawk-eyed attention to detail that later went into her bone fence.

When the building was finished, Jenny had room to spare. She rented out space on either side of her store to a dentist and a druggist. (We children never shopped there because Jenny could see us going in, so we cut across the square to the other drugstore for our cherry phosphates and ice cream.) Upstairs she put in four offices and rented them out to three lawyers and the probate judge.

Jenny's tenants soon learned that she was a tough landlord. When the attorney, Mr. Hybard, sometimes fell behind in his rent, Jenny never went quietly up the stairs to talk with him about the matter. She was much too given to theatrics for that. Instead, Jenny went out front, stood at the edge of the street, and hollered up at his window: "Charley! Charley Hybard! Come to your window! Charley, I am going to give you just twenty-four hours to pay your rent. If you don't, then out you go. Do you hear me, Charley? OK, Charley. Hide behind your window shade. But just remember—twenty-four hours and no more, Charley!"

It was like Corrie, our Negro house servant, used to say, "Dat Miz Jenny is half crool to dem peoples dat rents her places. She treats dem like a little boy dat's ready to pull de legs offen a grasshopper."

Jenny ordered a covered porch built across the front of the store, taking up the entire sidewalk. She placed rocking chairs and plank benches there for people to sit on and rest. Jenny figured this would help business. And it did, too; she usually had a good crowd out there. Sometimes if things threatened to get a little unruly, Jenny would start walking back and forth in front of her store, thumping the metal tip of her umbrella on the wooden sidewalk. This was always her sign that she meant business. The troublemakers would quickly slide off their seats and slither away like snakes in the grass. She would never take guff from anyone, no matter how big or important they were. The front of Jenny's store was always like a theater. Her shows never ceased to amaze us. We never knew what to expect next.

Eventually, the inside of the store became the dream of any young girl. As you came through the front door, there was a huge showcase that covered about twelve feet of wall and was filled with perfumes and expensive cosmetics. Next there was a long counter with yard measures cut into the wood. Behind the counter were shelves holding stacks and stacks of calicoes, solid-colored percales, and bolts of cloth of every description—stripes, dots, and figures. On the floor were bins that overflowed with lace, embroidery, rickrack braid in bright, bold colors, and soutache braid in gold, silver, and brilliant red. Against the opposite wall were cases filled with Vanity Fair silk-undergarments, and silk stockings hung from the wall behind. Jenny's pride was her front picture window that she had shipped in from New Orleans. The top border of the window was actually cut glass, large diamond-shaped fans that appeared to explode in the sunlight. In front of the store a large sign in bold black letters edged in gold announced: "V. H. & C. E. FAULK MERCANTILE CO." The "C. E." stood for Caroline Elizabeth; Jenny had forced Callie to quit her job as a teacher to work in her store.

Of course, all this was still a few years down the road in 1900, when Jenny started construction. But she was ambitious and never had any doubts about her eventual success.

It was the custom in Monroe County for the farmers to come into town on Saturday afternoons. While they bought their supplies, their wives shopped. Saturday was always Jenny's busiest day in the store. The women loved to sit on the benches in front and catch up on the latest gossip.

Jenny had a separate entrance for "colored." (This was typical of many women's shops in the South at the time.) Jenny never allowed the Negroes to try on any hats, dresses, or coats.

They had to buy their clothes right off the rack, and nothing they bought could ever be returned.

About the same time Jenny built her store, she also built the large, rambling frame house that would be her home—and Truman's—for so many years. Samantha, Callie, Sook, and Bud all settled with her in Monroeville. After Jenny moved the family to town, the old Faulk Plantation house went to rack and ruin. No one lived there. None of the family was sentimental about the place. After all, it was associated with too many painful memories, too many years of hardship, poverty, and backbreaking labor. So they simply moved out and left the old house to the mice and the elements. Sharecroppers in the area stripped away what they needed for building materials. By the time I was a young girl, little remained except four columns standing like lonely sentinels above the foundations and piles of debris.

Jenny thus made her home into a refuge for her mother, two sisters, and brother. Her own personal pleasures always came second to her responsibilities to her family and business. She never married, but she did have her lovers. One was Albert Godchaux, the antiques dealer from New Orleans who bought all the Faulk Plantation furnishings. Soon afterward he became Jenny's lover and benefactor. (Who knows? He probably lent her much of the money she needed to buy her land and construct her store and house.) Jenny always spoke highly of Mr. Godchaux, saying he was "a true Southern gentleman." She admired him for his distinguished looks, elegant manners, and patience and guidance in her own business affairs.

Jenny handled her affair with Mr. Godchaux with discretion and good taste. He was married, and his family lived in New Orleans. Jenny never had any aspirations for marriage, however, so the relationship proved perfect for each of them. Jenny frequently traveled around the country on buying trips, and the two often arranged to be together in another city for their interludes away from the prying eyes of their families.

On rare occasions Mr. Godchaux would visit Monroeville. Jenny always kept their meetings formal, so very few people there suspected. I met him first when I was a girl. He was a huge man, well over six feet tall, with exceptionally broad shoulders. He gave the impression of enormous strength, both physical and emotional. His eyes were a dark brown, and he had a head of wavy, iron-gray hair. He was slightly on the paunchy side, but an elegant dresser.

To me then the most fascinating thing about Mr. Godchaux was his watch. He carried a large, expensive gold pocket watch that hung at the end of a long gold chain. He draped it over the front of his vest and tucked the watch into his pocket. When he pulled out the watch, it was as though a large piece of ice had suddenly shattered, flinging the rays of sunlight in all directions. The watch's back was studded with diamonds. The hands pointed to numbers made out of rubies. To me, Mr. Godchaux's watch was like an emissary from a world of warrior kings, distressed princesses, and enchanted courts. He told us that he had bought it in France.

In fact, it was on that visit that Mr. Godchaux presented Jenny with a pair of small gold scissors studded with precious stones. She treasured her gift. After that, Jenny almost always wore the gold scissors on a long chain attached to her bodice in the manner of a Mlle. Demerest of New York who had made a fortune designing and selling dress patterns. Jenny carried the patterns in her store and had been quite impressed by stories of her charm, grace, poise, and dignity, which she read in magazines. The patterns always showed a picture of Mlle. Demerest with a small pair of scissors attached to her bodice, a bauble suggesting her trade.

The last time I saw Mr. Godchaux was in 1930 on Jenny's fifty-seventh birthday. Jenny had the party catered from Mobile with an elegant tiered cake topped with sugar flowers of violet and pink. Age had not robbed Jenny of her beauty and presence. She stood out in the crowded room like the queen she was, her dress a cloud of whiteness that billowed out in a great bell shape from her still tiny waist. She slowly fingered a long strand of amethysts around her neck as she sat *tête-à-tête* with Mr. Godchaux.

Jenny had other lovers, I suppose, although we never knew for certain about them. In the front yard hidden beneath the rosebushes was a small tombstone that read simply, "ONE DAY OLD." Jenny would never answer our questions about it. But Callie, her sister, whispered—perhaps with more spite than truth—that it was the grave of a stillborn illegitimate child Jenny had had by a lover in St. Louis, where she went often on buying trips.

Corrie, our Negro house servant, summed it up best of all: "Miz Jenny is whats I calls a high-vitality female."

Callie, Jenny's younger sister, had been a schoolteacher until Jenny forced her to quit to help out in the store. Like a boa constrictor crushing its prey, the older sister completely dominated the younger. Even though she had been baptized Caroline Elizabeth, she was known throughout her life as Callie, a name she detested, insisting it sounded like the name of a Negro maid. This was Jenny's name for her and it stuck. Whatever name Jenny used, the rest of the family and town took up. So poor Callie was denied even the dignity of her own name.

Callie was a severe woman with gray eyes as hard as rifle balls. She had a precise, thin upper lip and a round chin that always quivered violently just before the tears came in the many confrontations with her sister. Her hair was coal black, and she wore it bobbed all her life. She had tiny feet that she always pampered in later years with shoes of the softest leather. Her waist was the envy of many a younger woman. Bud would often tell her, "Not a girl in the whole town has a waist like yours, Caroline. Why, a man could get his two hands around it with plenty of room to spare!" Bud, by the way, was the only one to defy Jenny on the matter of Callie's name and call her Caroline.

Callie was the only truly religious member of our family. She went to church every Sunday, but Jenny attended when it suited her. Callie would often call upon the Lord to save her from grief at the hands of her sister. "The Lord take care of Jenny and her evil tongue," she would say. "God isn't going to make me live this way forever. He'll take me away someday!"

When Callie was eighteen years old, she began to teach school. She had acquired a teacher's certificate from a "normal" school. In those days professional requirements for teachers were virtually nonexistent. Callie went to work in a one-room rural schoolhouse near Franklin, Alabama, teaching several grades and all subjects.

There was too little love in Callie for her ever to have been a good teacher. The parents of the children disliked her prim and arrogant attitude, and the children hated her. Callie did mean things sometimes, such as sending her dirtier pupils home to their parents (probably poor white sharecroppers) with neatly printed signs around their necks that read, "Wash this boy's ears. They have enough dirt in them to grow corn."

When my mother died and Jenny took me, Lillie Mae, and the rest of my family into her home, Callie welcomed us in a cool, restrained way. In sharp contrast, Bud and Sook were happy to have us move in. I don't think any of us ever really warmed up to Callie. She never mistreated us, but we always knew that she merely tolerated us.

Callie's fate, her burden in life, was not to be able to escape Jenny. They were bound together for life in a strange dependence that ate at both of them. Jenny hated her sister for her weakness. Callie hated Jenny for her strength. Every effort of Callie's to establish some sort of life independent of Jenny was deliberately frustrated. Once Callie developed an infatuation for the family doctor, a married man. Jenny put an end to Callie's fake fainting spells. No more romance. The last thing she wanted was a family scandal in Monroeville.

"God, how I hate that Jenny," Callie would say after each humiliating encounter with her older sister. "If only I had the strength to leave and make a living for myself." But she never could, not even after Jenny horsewhipped her fiancé out of town.

When I was growing up, one of the most frequently told stories in Monroeville was how Jenny had run Callie's beau out of town years before. Mr. Buck—that was the only name people knew him by—was a traveling salesman from Atlanta. He was a short man, with bowed legs and a somewhat oversized head. What he lacked in looks he made up in manner. Mr. Buck was a good-natured fellow with a fine wit and an excellent sense of humor. He always dressed in an expensive, if flamboyant, style, his shirt and tie exactly right.

Somehow an attraction developed between Mr. Buck and Callie, although the latter's restrained manner and dress would certainly have suggested to a more sensitive man that she was a rather repressed woman. Or perhaps Mr. Buck detected in Callie a desperation to get away from her sister at any cost.

As soon as Jenny learned about the liaison, she hired a private detective in Atlanta to check out Mr. Buck. In the meantime Callie announced her engagement. The detective discovered that Mr. Buck's business career had been somewhat checkered. He had once been the manager of a traveling Chautauqua and at one time had owned half interest in a two-headed pig that was popular at the county fairs. But the report also revealed a damning truth—Mr. Buck had a wife and six "snot-nosed kids" in Atlanta.

It so happened that Mr. Buck was in town when Jenny received the report from her detective. Jenny was in the process of closing her store for the day when she saw Mr. Buck emerge from the old Deese Hotel across the square and head for her store to pick up Callie. Jenny gave him a few minutes, then rushed out, buggy whip in hand, to rescue her erring sister from a would-be bigamist.

Jenny cracked the whip and shouted curses at the surprised Mr. Buck. "I don't like a lying weasel," she hollered. "You low-down goat. I'll turn you inside out and then cut your damn pecker off."

The townspeople on the street looked on in amazement. Mr. Buck jumped back abruptly, startled. Then he headed for his hotel. But Jenny got in one good blow, bringing her whip down sharply across his face, drawing blood from the corner of his mouth. Not one of the spectators dared to stop Jenny.

The street was utterly silent. No sound was to be heard, except that of Mr. Buck's steps as he retraced his path to the hotel. A stunned Callie stood in shock on the sidewalk in front of Jenny's store. She turned slowly and then went inside. The time of flowers, walks along the river, and whispered endearments was gone forever. For Callie the future spread out as blank as a prairie.

Nancy, or Sook as she was known to the family, was Jenny's older sister and Truman's favorite. She exerted a profound influence, not always constructive, on the young Truman. He later immortalized her in three of his most famous stories: *The Grass Harp*, *A Christmas Memory*, and *A Thanksgiving Visitor*. Sook was the kind of person who loved all living things. All stray animals, stray children, anything in need, became a part of her. And in 1924 when the baby Truman was brought to Jenny's home in Monroeville, it was Sook who cared for him as though he were a gift from heaven. He filled a void in her life and gave it meaning.

Sook was all innocence, unable to adapt to the demands of the world at large. She possessed a childlike perception of life that she never lost. Sook was the most fragile, dependent, and vulnerable of William's children. Jenny's house really was her refuge in a more immediate way than it was for the others.

John Byron, or Bud as everyone called him, was the older brother. He was a good-natured, kind man but weak and unable to assert himself in the family, a failure by the traditional definitions of the word. Bud's pride was the 600 acres he had inherited from his father's plantation. He never worked a day in his life, and he never did anything with his land except let Sylvester, an ancient black man, sharecrop part of the farm to grow a little cotton.

Jenny allowed Bud only one responsibility in her home. He was to act as host and master of the house, but only at the dining-room table. There he sat at the head and carved the roasts and fowls that came in from the kitchen. Bud said the blessing, served the plates, and kept a sharp eye on our behavior. In all important matters, however, especially those involving business, ·Jenny rigidly excluded Bud, never even asking his advice.

There were two other people in our household in 1924 when the baby Truman came to live with us: Little Bit, our black cook, and Corrie, the black house servant. Both had lived on the premises for as long as I could remember and had become by then an integral part of the family circle.

Sook, Bud, Little Bit, and Corrie were all fascinating people who in their different ways influenced Truman as a boy. Much more will be said about each later.

When Truman arrived in Jenny's home in 1924, he was the fifth generation of Faulks to find refuge under her roof. If I had to fix on the single most important characteristic of Jenny, it would be her intense loyalty to her family. Everything else was secondary. When she died in 1958, Jenny stipulated in her will that the big house in Monroeville not be sold for twenty years. Rather it was to be kept as a refuge for any family member who fell upon hard times and needed shelter. And so it has remained, even until today.

CHAPTER TWO

Lillie Mae

IN THE ENTRANCE HALL of Jenny's big frame house hung a comparatively small portrait of a young woman dressed in a low-cut crimson silk bodice that revealed an almost indecent expanse of bare breast. Pale gold hair framed the perfect face. The skin of her neck and shoulders suggested something of the velvety softness of magnolia petals. It had been painted, as I recall, by an artist of some local renown in Mobile and was strikingly lifelike. You sensed that the woman might at any moment step down from the ugly gilded frame and with a swish and swirl of her silk skirt escort you into the nearby parlor. This was Truman's mother, Lillie Mae Faulk Persons. She always liked to think of herself as a Greek siren luring men to their destruction, but the truth was much more prosaic. Lillie Mae was more like the moth trapped on the inside of a windowpane that in a mindless frenzy beats its wings to tatters in a desperate attempt to escape.

How Lillie Mae, I, and the other members of our family ended up in Jenny's house of refuge is a story of some length that needs to be told here, for Truman's story is finally the story of his family back through several generations and cannot be understood without that background. We Southerners (far more than our northern brethren) have always had a keen appreciation of the importance of place and history as determining factors in our lives, especially those of us raised in small Southern towns before 1950. Robert Penn Warren, another Southern writer, wrote years ago in his novel *Band of Angels:* "You live through time, but that piece of time is not only your own life, it is the summing-up of all the other lives that are simultaneous with yours." And, he might have added, "previous to yours." For we Southerners have never been able to leave the past alone. We are a ghost-ridden people, as William Faulkner understood.

Lillie Mae's and my father, James Arthur Faulk, called Arthur, was born November 8, 1886, in Monroe County, Alabama, the son of Seaborn Jackson Faulk and Ida Electra Henderson. Seaborn was a prosperous man with a plantation outside Monroeville and a resort hotel in Bluff Springs, Florida, about forty-five miles away. A second son, Henderson Wingate, came along soon afterward. Ida died suddenly in 1888. Despondent over the death of his wife, Seaborn started drinking and gambling compulsively. Soon he sold off his resort hotel, only to lose that money at the gaming tables. In a short time he had mortgaged his plantation and household goods. Things went from bad to worse, and he lost his land.

Seaborn soon moved his family to Laurel, Mississippi, where he had a turpentine mill he had won at the gaming table. He had hoped to use the mill as a means of rebuilding his position in society, but it turned out to be a marginal operation and was later taken over by one of the laborers. In late 1893 Seaborn died in Laurel, a broken and ill man. Samantha, a distant cousin, could not attend the funeral and instead sent Bud to Laurel with instructions to bring the two orphaned boys back to Faulk's Plantation. He found the boys slaving away in the turpentine mill under the supervision of a pistol-toting former partner of Seaborn's, who made them work ten hours a day alongside the men in the woods, tapping pine trees and collecting turpentine resin. Times were hard for Samantha's family, but they never hesitated to take the two small children into their home.

Samantha quickly became quite attached to Arthur and Henderson and flatly refused to allow them to work in the cotton fields. She always felt that the horrible experience they had had in the turpentine mill was more than enough for any child to have to bear in life.

Bud always told us that Popper (our children's nickname for our father) was a wild, unruly child who was intensely protective of his sickly little brother, Henderson. He had a savage temper, and it took very little to get him to start swinging. Bud loved to tell us (for our Popper died when we were quite young) the story of a battle royal that our father fought with the town bully when he was about nine.

When farmers and plantation owners came into Monroeville on Saturday afternoon to buy their groceries and other supplies, their children usually gathered in the square for fun and games. On this particular afternoon Popper and another boy had drawn squares in the dirt for a game of hopscotch. The town bully, Lem Peavy, a sixteen-year-old with fiery red hair and small squinty eyes, came up. Lem took his foot and rubbed out the dirt squares, taunting Popper. "Look a-yonder at shorty Faulk, now, would you?"

"You go to hell!" Popper retorted.

"Watch yore tongue, boy," Lem shot back. "You ain't old enough to cuss. Little boys who ain't no bigger than a chicken mite need to mind their manners when they is round their elders."

Before Lem could say another word, Popper jumped him. He may have been much smaller and younger than the bully, but he was tougher, faster, and meaner than many boys twice his age. Popper was on Lem like a cornered bobcat protecting its kittens—biting, scratching, kicking, and pounding him. Lem never knew what hit him. He dropped to his knees, bleeding from his nose and mouth. Popper kept at him. He was never one to yield the advantage once he had it.

Shouts of "Fight! Fight! Fight!" echoed across the square. A large crowd quickly gathered. Bud stood on the edge, watching the brawl. One of the men called out to him, "Bud, stop this fight. Arthur just may hurt Lem bad."

"Hell, no," Bud hollered back. "That boy needs the shit kicked out of him just once to teach him a lesson. Then maybe he'll stop bullying kids half his age." Bud turned back to the fight. "Go to it, Arthur," he shouted. "Teach that bastard some manners."

Popper learned early to fight his way through life.

Popper's great love was horses. There were a couple at the plantation, and every chance he had he saddled up and galloped across the fields. When he was twelve years old, he got a job in town at the stables, currying, feeding, and cleaning up after the horses. He worked hard and saved every cent he made. Popper looked around him at the hard life everyone led on the Faulk Plantation, and he swore while very young that someday he would put poverty behind him and be a rich man.

When Popper was seventeen, he got another job, carrying the mail by horseback from Monroeville to Mexia and Brewton. The trips weren't easy. The roads were rough, and there were few bridges. Often he had to ford a river or creek in the cold early morning. It was on one of those trips that Popper saw his first lynching. As a child I heard him tell the story a dozen times, and it made a great impression on me.

One evening while Popper was carrying the mail, he crossed through a small covered bridge, the clomping of his horse's hooves making a loud and eerie sound in the night. As he came out of the bridge, Popper was suddenly confronted by a hooded man in a white robe, holding a pistol, who grabbed his reins and ordered him off his horse. Popper was not one to argue with a pointed pistol, so he did as the man said. He looked off into the woods nearby and saw a group of hooded men carrying torches.

"Boy," the hooded figure said, "we are about to have ourselves a lynching. You ever seen a man hanged?"

"No, sir," answered Popper. "But I'm carrying the U.S. Mail, and I can't stop."

"Boys," the figure yelled to his friends, "he says he's carrying the mail and can't be stopped. Don't that beat all?"

"Hell, it's a lynching," another hooded figure hollered back. "We're going to stretch a nigger's neck. You stay and see justice done."

"What did the nigger do?" Popper asked.

"Do? Why, boy, that nigger fooled around with a white girl, that's what he did."

"Well, that's different," Popper said. "I guess I can spare the time."

He followed the hooded figure who had first stopped him to a large tree on one side of the road. A knotted rope had already been thrown over one limb. Several other hooded men dragged a black boy, probably no older than Popper himself, out of the shadows to the tree. He was covered with blood. Popper could see where his captors had nicked his skin in dozens of places with the points of their pocket knives. His shirt and pants were drenched in his blood.

One man took out some rope and knotted the black boy's hands behind his back while two others held him tightly. Then they fitted the noose over his head and fixed it snugly around his neck.

"Fer Gawd's sake, white mens, please don't hang me to dat tree," the boy pleaded pathetically. "Oh, please don't, white boss, for Gawd's sake, please don't."

None of the men appeared to listen. The other end of the rope was fastened around the pommel of a saddle. Then the horse moved back a few steps, putting tension on the rope and forcing the black boy to stand on his toes to keep his balance.

"Cut that nigger's balls off first before we hang him," the leader ordered.

The boy thrashed about, kicking frantically, but it did no

good. Two men pinioned him while another stripped his pants off, took a long hunting knife, and with a swift, slashing blow castrated the helpless Negro. Popper said later he thought you could have heard his shriek all the way back in Monroeville. Then they urged the horse forward and jerked him into the air. The body twisted and turned in the shadows of the flickering torches. Suddenly, the leader drew his pistol, pointed it at the writhing figure, and fired three shots into his body. Before they left, the group tied the rope to the tree trunk and left the dead black hanging there as a warning.

All the cruelty he had just witnessed nauseated Popper. He stumbled away into the darkness and vomited. Soon afterward he decided to quit the mail route.

By then Popper was married. He had met his wife on one of his trips to Mexia, where he regularly carried the mails. He had stayed overnight in the Hendrix house. The Hendrixes were an old family who had first come to this country about the time of the American Revolution. A Hendrix several generations back had made a small fortune by taking his slaves to Mammoth Cave, Kentucky, to mine saltpeter (used in making gunpowder) during the War of 1812. The Hendrix family was well established in the southwestern corner of Alabama.

Popper fell in love with Edna Marie, a shy girl who had just turned sixteen. Popper at the time was eighteen, not much over five feet tall, with a high forehead and a jawbone that looked so strong an ax couldn't break it. The two things he could call his own were a fine breeding horse and a fancy clock. Maybe because of that he was afraid Moses Hendrix would turn down his request for his daughter's hand in marriage. So Popper talked Edna Marie into eloping. One fine day in early 1904 they rode into Brewton and got married. He brought his bride back to Monroeville to the new house that Jenny had built in town.

Both Samantha and Jenny were upset that Popper had married so young—"without a pot to piss in," as Jenny put it. Samantha made my mother feel at home, however, because she knew the Hendrix family by name and reputation and felt, as she so often said, that "he could have done a lot worse."

My mother was a short woman, pretty in an unassuming way, who inclined toward plumpness in later years. She had dark brown eyes and hair the color of amber that set off a delicately molded face. Her father had been a minister at one time and enrolled her at a young age in a church school in Mobile. Edna Marie had never had reason to do hard work. Rather she had been taught to sew, embroider, and play the piano. My mother was a happy person, always singing, with a smile for everyone.

Jenny always said that my mother was so much in love that she made a complete fool of herself. Perhaps the contrast between the two was the bond—his reckless, wild, impetuous nature against her fine breeding and gentleness. They were an unlikely match, no doubt of it.

Popper quit his mail route and turned to horses, his second love after Edna Marie. He took what money he had saved and started buying horses. He went to Texas and New Mexico for many of them. Popper kept his herd outside town on a part of Bud's 600 acres. He roped off some pastureland, planted some rye and oats, and grazed his horses there. Within a few years Popper had established himself as one of the smartest and most successful horse traders in the whole state. He specialized in racehorses, breeding and selling them. He never raced them, and he never gambled on them, for he keenly remembered the horror stories of his father's gambling fever.

Popper and Edna Marie lived in Jenny's big house in Monroeville for the first three years of their marriage. Popper spent much of that time away in different parts of the South putting together his horse deals. Mother found company with Corrie (who even then worked for Jenny) and Sook in the big kitchen. She was an excellent cook. In later years when we girls were growing up, after our mother had gone to an early grave, both Sook and Corrie used to tell us about the glorious salads and the fresh apple pies that Edna Marie had put on the dining-room table.

One evening the family was relaxing in the parlor. Popper was away, looking at horses north of Montgomery. Mother sat sewing, quietly thrusting the needle back and forth. Suddenly, she looked up from her work and announced proudly, "We are going to have a child."

Jenny was distressed. "I'm going to tell you something, Edna, that you should know," she said. "By having a baby so soon you will hamstring Arthur for the rest of his life. You both are too young. And Arthur needs all his energies for his business. You can't be having a baby now."

"The Lord will provide," Mother insisted stubbornly.

"Provide what?" Jenny wanted to know. "Collard greens and purple turnips?"

Of course, never having been married herself, Jenny could not appreciate how easily children came along. Edna Marie was delivered of her first child, Lillie Mae, on January 29, 1905, in Jenny's house with the aid of Anna Stabler, a Negro woman who was midwife to half the white people born in Monroeville.

Through some astute horse swapping, Popper managed to get together some cash. He purchased 160 acres of land near Bud's fields. In this way he could continue to graze his herd on Bud's rich pastureland. Then he built a house for his family. It was narrow but deep in the back with rooms off a long hallway. There was a good-size parlor, so that Mother could have a piano. Popper could not afford the luxury of indoor plumbing. Corrie's advice on setting up the privy was "Don't never build no outhus near no chinaberry tree 'cause de rattlesnakes will crawl up dem holes."

All the relatives and their friends from church got together to give the couple a "pounding." This was a custom of helping out newlyweds by giving them old furniture, used linen, whatever people no longer needed that might still be of use. Many a couple in Monroeville got their start that way. Popper and Mother ended up with a chest of drawers made out of white pine with a wax inlay (all handmade and kept as long as I can remember), a pie cupboard, a jelly safe, knives and forks, and a hodgepodge of ill-assorted odds and ends.

Eventually, five more children were born to James Arthur and Edna Marie Faulk. They were Seaborn Jackson (January 20, 1907), Mary Ida (December 31, 1908), me, Edna Marie (March 13, 1911), George (May 31, 1913—he died within a few months), and finally Lucille (August 13, 1915).

After I was born, Popper moved us into a larger house in town only about five blocks from Jenny's house. He hired a Negro named Homer as a full-time handyman to help Mother out. Poor Homer. He fell victim to Popper's violent temper. When I was a small baby, Popper put me on the back porch one day and told Homer to keep an eye on me. He was slack in his duties, and I stayed in the sun too long and blistered badly. My father was so enraged that he picked up a heavy wooden yoke and brought it crashing down on the head of the negligent Negro, crushing his skull and spilling his brains out into the grass. In those days, of course, the sheriff would never have dared to press charges.

My father's life was a short one, filled with hard work, success, and an early death caused by his reckless, impulsive ways.

It was late March 1916 when Popper was training a wild stallion. I had just turned five, but the memory of that day remains clear even today. At the back of our house Popper had built a large oval pen where he broke his wild horses so that they could be ridden. I stood on the fence and watched him that day. Popper was a great rider; he could handle just about any horse that came his way. That day he was working with a magnificent white stallion, riding him around and around the pen. Suddenly, the horse reared back and then kicked, pitching his rider over his head. Popper struck the ground hard and lay still. The big white stallion reared again, nostrils flaring, snorting loudly, and brought his hooves down hard again and again on poor Popper's prostrate body. He missed his head but crushed one of his arms.

One of the Negro hands hollered for Mama to get a revolver quick. She grabbed the revolver out of the bottom of the flour bin where she kept it (away from the hands of us children) and rushed to the back steps. She handed the gun to Mr. Metz, a man who had heard the commotion and rushed over. Mr. Metz fired one shot into the air to sound an emergency—an old custom in our town. It was like an S.O.S. Within a few minutes a dozen men and boys arrived at our corral to help.

The stallion had started galloping around the pen again, stopping occasionally to snort and paw the air with his front hooves. Popper still lay unconscious where he had hit the ground.

Mr. Metz opened the gate. "You other men do what you can to distract that horse, so that I can get Faulk and drag him out." Everyone shouted as loudly as they could, shook blankets, and fired the pistol in the air to scare the stallion away from Popper. Mr. Metz rushed in, grabbed him by the feet, and dragged him as quickly as he could through the gate.

I remember Mama holding my hand so tightly that it turned purple. The men carried Popper nearer the house and laid him gently on the ground. His face was blotched with large purple patches. His breath was short and thick. Blood dripped out of his mouth. Mother told me much later that she knew then and there that Popper was going to die.

A neighbor drove Popper to a hospital in Mobile. There the doctors discovered that his spine had been crushed in the fall and he had suffered massive internal injuries. Six weeks later he came home. He died in his wife's arms on May 7, 1916.

We were all at Popper's bedside when he died. Mother became hysterical. "I can't give Arthur up, I can't let him go," she wailed. "Arthur, answer me, please answer. Don't leave me."

Jenny took Mother by the arm and led her gently from the room. "Edna, he can't hear you anymore," she said quietly. "Come now. I'm taking you and all the children to my house. I want you to rest. I will take care everything here."

Jenny did just that and much more. Within a few days Mama and we five children were all installed in Jenny's home. I am certain that she had realized for some time that Popper would not make it and had made plans to move us to her house. Jenny must have known that Mama could never have handled by herself the details of Popper's business or the care of us children. We never returned to our old house. Jenny sold the house, the farm, and all the horses. The only thing she kept was a beautiful leather saddle that Popper had had custom made several years before. Later Jenny gave this to my only brother, Seaborn Jackson.

My mother never questioned or even asked about anything Jenny did. She simply accepted it. Jenny was always so much more dynamic and effectual than Mama ever could be that she had the poor woman quite intimidated. She never really recovered from the blow of Popper's death. On May 9, 1919, Mother herself died unexpectedly of a cerebral hemorrhage, exactly three years and two days after Popper's death. I still think that as the anniversary of Popper's death approached, Mama simply willed her own death so that she could be with her husband again.

Lillie Mae, Mary Ida, and I continued to live with Jenny. Lucille and Seaborn went to live with Uncle Howard and Aunt Abeygale. Jenny had wanted to keep the five of us together under her roof, but Uncle Howard insisted on splitting us up. When Mama died, Lillie Mae was fourteen years old, and she, unlike Mary Ida or me, resented having to live with Jenny. For some reason she suddenly assumed a "mother" role with us other two children. It never suited her nature, but I think she felt compelled to try to do something because she was the oldest. At first Lillie Mae helped us dress for school, and she did our hair. But as time went on, her maternal responsibilities gradually dropped by the wayside, one by one. She began to feel cheated and to complain that her attentions to Mary Ida and me did not allow her to devote enough time to herself. Lillie Mae always felt that our parents did not have the "right" to die. She said this many times. And she began to develop a bitterness and belligerence that was characteristic of her until the end of her life.

The clashes between Jenny and Lillie Mae started at an early date and lasted a lifetime. My sister was a problem child even then—headstrong, disobedient, independent, and boy crazy. She tried to dress and act as though she were six years older. In fact, Lillie Mae was a flapper even before flappers became popular. She loved to go into Jenny's room and get into her jewelry box. She would pull out ropes of pearls and hang them around her neck and put gold bracelets on each arm. Then she would unbutton her dress in front and dab perfume between her breasts and under her arms. Thus decked out, Lillie Mae would sashay boldly out the front door on her way to school. Jenny would grab her by her skirt and drag her back inside the house, stripping off the jewelry.

"Get back in here this minute, young lady!" Jenny would holler at Lillie Mae. "By all that is holy, you won't leave my house looking like some trash from Rooktown. If I see you again in public with paint on your lips and stinking like a nigger from all that perfume, you will live to regret it. Do you understand me, Lillie Mae?"

"You're not my mother, Jenny Faulk. You can't boss me like that. I ain't your nigger. Don't tell me what to do. I'm grown up," Lillie Mae would scream back, tears welling up in her eyes.

"I may not be your mother, girl, but I am your guardian,"

Jenny would insist. "I put food in your stomach, clothes on your body, and a roof over your head. So you show me some respect."

"God, I hate you, Jenny Faulk," Lillie Mae would cry, going to her room and slamming the door so hard that it almost jumped off its hinges.

Bud came into the front hallway. He had heard the entire exchange back in the kitchen. "Jenny," he said, "go a little easy. Don't you know they're hurting? Wait at least until they get used to the idea of being without a father and a mother and look on us as their kin and protector."

"Shut up, you soft-hearted old fool," Jenny snapped, and stormed out of the house to her store.

Lillie Mae was always fond of clothes. Jenny gave us almost anything we wanted from the store and bought our dressier clothing in St. Louis. We always had the best of everything.

Even as a teenage girl, Lillie Mae liked to show off her body. When Jenny gave her a dress or a blouse with long sleeves and a high neck, Lillie Mae would get the scissors almost at once. She would cut the sleeves and neck off, plunging the neckline in front to a deep *V*. Then she would take the mutilated garment to the store and have Jenny's seamstress fix everything to her liking.

When Jenny learned what had happened, she would be furious. And another argument would begin, as the two of them squared off like a cat and a dog spoiling for a good fight.

"What in the name of heaven do you think you are doing, young lady?" Jenny would demand. "Cutting up your clothes that I paid good money for. Have you taken leave of your senses, child?"

And then Jenny would hold up the blouse she had gotten from the seamstress. "Just look at that," she would say. "Why in God's name did you cut the neck out of this pure silk blouse?"

"Because, Miss Jenny Faulk, I am not an old woman like you. I do not need to hide the wrinkles on *my* neck, like some people in this house. I want to pick out my own clothes from here on."

"That suits me to a tee. Then you don't get any." And Jenny gave the blouse to a Negro girl in town, so that Lillie Mae would be certain to see it now and then.

Corrie had her own explanation of why Lillie Mae acted as she did.

"My, my," Corrie would say. "Many a tear will be shed over dat chile. I'se warnin' yo, Miz Jenny. Dat Lillie Mae got thin blood. An' thin blood runs to wickedness."

"Mind your own business, Corrie."

"I'se gwine do dat, Miz Jenny. But dat's de Gawd's truf."

Jenny would live to see Corrie proved correct.

Lillie Mae continued to be a problem for Jenny. She was disobedient, surly, and ungrateful. At sixteen she was a spoiled child in the body of a woman. She plucked her eyebrows, rouged the dimples on her knees, and walked with a twitch in her buttocks that mesmerized the boys in her school. Sometimes she wore an ankle chain—a "slave bracelet," she called it—that an older boy had given her.

Even as a young girl, Lillie Mae shaped her character and mannerisms to attract men. She directed all her actions, unconscious as well as conscious ones, toward attracting a mate. She learned early in life that she could easily have her way with a man by being adorable and desirable. Lillie Mae was a passionate woman and did little to censure her instincts, a fact that outraged and frustrated Jenny's sense of propriety. I remember that after her bath an older Lillie Mae loved to stroll naked around her bedroom, admiring her body in the mirror. Then she would reluctantly put on her underwear, including brassieres that set off her breasts to full advantage.

And Lillie Mae could be cruel, puncturing someone else's happiness with a sharp remark, smiling as she said it. She could be kind and reassuring one moment and then humiliate you in the next. I recall one dreadful Sunday dinner in 1925 with all the family present around the big dining-room table when Lillie Mae turned on me. She shocked the group by telling them I was so stupid I could not even keep my Kotex pad on.

"Why, the other day when we were in Mobile, clumsy Tiny dropped hers in public view. Right there on the sidewalk—down it fell," Lillie Mae revealed. "And then she had the uncommon sense to try and pick it up. I had to jerk her along, kick the nasty rag into the gutter, and hurry her on. Isn't that the most foolish thing you ever heard?"

No one I ever met could twist happiness into pain as quickly as Lillie Mae. "I swear, she mus' of had a evil spirit rockin' her cradle," Corrie would say. "Lillie Mae will *never* be content. She's born greedy for mens an' money."

Lillie Mae loved to visit the big house of Grandmother Hendrix located outside Mexia on a high hill overlooking a beautiful stream. It was there that we children learned how to ride horses. Lillie Mae loved horses and rode with ease and grace. This was a talent she must have inherited from our father.

I recall one visit in the summer of 1922 when Lillie Mae and I stood outside the small family cemetery that Grandmother Hendrix had just to one side of her house. A fancy grilled wrought-iron fence, imported from France, surrounded a small collection of simple marble headstones and tall monuments.

Suddenly, Lillie Mae said to me, "Doesn't the thought of no God, no hereafter, just paralyze you?"

"But there is a God," I insisted. "What do you mean, Lillie Mae?"

"I don't think so," Lillie Mae went on quietly. "If there were, why did He take Popper and Mother from us so young?"

She thought some more.

"Damn, there is so much hypocrisy in church, Tiny. How can you stand it? Just look at Uncle Howard. He's always telling us about the importance of a good Christian upbringing. That old sot keeps himself a nigger woman in Rooktown, blows all his money on moonshine on Saturday night, and then is the first one in the front pew in church on Sunday morning. If anyone lit a match near him, the whole church would explode!"

I was always skeptical about how much of an atheist Lillie Mae really was. It sometimes seemed to me that what really bothered her were the restraints that Christian morality would impose on her actions. Like many self-indulgent people, Lillie Mae resented anyone or anything that tried to limit her pleasures. "We have to act out our emotions, Tiny," she would tell me in great seriousness. "Never be afraid to seize the moment. We may not get tomorrow. Look at what happened to poor Popper."

Jenny finally threw up her hands in despair over Lillie Mae and sent her away to Schoffner's School for Young Ladies in Brewton, Alabama. There, Jenny hoped, she would be taught all the social graces of a Southern belle. Lillie Mae was sixteen at the time. The plan didn't work. Lillie Mae was as unruly and outrageous at the fancy finishing school as she was at home in Monroeville. She slipped out of her bedroom window at night for dates in town with her boyfriends, and she was discovered smoking in her room. This was strictly against the rules. When they caught her, Lillie Mae was sitting by her window and blowing her cigarette smoke out, so that it wouldn't smell up her room. After a few months Mr. Schoffner drover over to Monroeville to visit Jenny. The two of them argued for the longest time, Mr. Schoffner insisting that Lillie Mae was corrupting the morals of the other girls at his school, Jenny insisting that if he just gave her one more chance she would come around. But Mr. Schoffner was adamant. Jenny finally withdrew Lillie Mae from his school.

Lillie Mae returned to Monroeville and graduated high school there. She was always a mediocre student. Years later, after she had married Joe Capote, a Cuban of Spanish descent, she would laugh when the subject of education came up and say, "When I was in school, I managed to pick up enough math to balance my checkbook and enough Spanish to get my Latin."

By the time Lillie Mae was a senior in high school she had come to think of herself as a heartless siren who toyed with men, ruined them, and then tossed them aside. She always found some excuse to get to Mobile whenever one of Theda Bara's new films opened. The Hollywood Vamp was her idol. Later, when the twenties finally caught up with the South, Lillie Mae chucked Theda Bara for Clara Bow. She was the first woman in Monroeville to buy herself a fringed skirt that came up to her knees. It was very daring at the time and created quite a sensation. When Lillie Mae did the Charleston, she was a blur of red chiffon and fringe. By then Jenny had long since given up trying to impose some sort of dress code on her. The young men, of course, loved it, and Lillie Mae collected beaux the way some people collect stamps.

None of those men exerted more than a momentary pull on Lillie Mae's heart strings. Her first true love, and her only enduring passion, was for a Creek Indian by the name of Tecumseh (Teshu for short) Waterford who lived on a reservation in the nearby community of Clairborne. He was two years older than Lillie Mae. She had first seen him when they were both much younger. For a brief time Teshu had attended school in Monroeville. Then he moved to Florida to live with relatives and finish high school.

Their attraction began to develop in 1921 when Lillie Mae was about to turn sixteen. Sook made a trip to one of the Creek settlements outside Clairborne where she went periodically to purchase some herbs. Lillie Mae, bored and restless, went along. On that trip she met Teshu again, and her life changed.

Teshu was a large man, powerfully built, with thick black hair and a voluptuous mouth. He was not friendly; he talked to no white more than was absolutely necessary. His speech was monosyllabic. For Lillie Mae he had an appealing timidity that could probably be traced to his Indian heritage. He was at first utterly indifferent to Lillie Mae's charms and beauty. She was quite taken aback. This both bothered and intrigued her.

When Lillie Mae made the trips to Clairborne with Sook, she always saw Teshu, usually standing alone on a high bluff overlooking the village where he could both see and be seen. "The wind made my skirt billow way up, so he could see what beautiful legs and thighs I have," Lillie Mae would tell me later. (She was a shameless braggart when it came to her own body.) "But later—I swear to you, Tiny—he looks right through me as though I am not even there, turns his back, and walks away."

"Oh, Lillie Mae," I would say in encouragement. "Don't worry. Who wants an old Indian, anyway?"

"I do," Lillie Mae would answer, emphatically. Teshu was different from all the others. He was not only handsome and sexy. He was exotic—and forbidden fruit, being an Indian. (In our South at that time, for a white woman to see an Indian socially was not quite as bad as for her to take a Negro as a lover, but it was definitely something no respectable woman could do and still keep her good reputation in the community.)

"Lillie Mae, stay away from that Indian," I warned her. "If Jenny finds out about this, you will be in real trouble. She'd practically kill you, and you know it!"

"She's not going to find out," Lillie Mae insisted. "Sook doesn't even know the time of day, let alone about Teshu. Well, I'll just keep going to Clairborne with her. I'll get that Indian if it is the last thing I do."

And so Lillie Mae returned again and again to the Creek reservation on the banks of the Alabama River. The Indians still maintained many of their tribal customs at that time, and Lillie Mae was fascinated by what she observed. Because of Sook (who enjoyed a close friendship with the shaman), she was invited to several of the village's feasts. For the Creeks almost any significant occasion was cause for a feast, whether it was the completion of a new house, the naming of a child, a marriage, or perhaps merely honoring the dead. At the start of all these feasts the shaman would elevate a portion of the food to be eaten to the four cardinal points of the compass and then drop it, properly blessed, into the fire. During this offering of thanks for the gift of food, everyone present would remain silent and motionless. Once Lillie Mae and Sook were present at a Creek harvest festival and watched the Indians do the Green Corn Dance. New corn was eaten, new fires kindled, and new garments were worn. All past enmities were forgiven.

Lillie Mae, however, refused to lose sight of her major objective—to get Teshu interested in her. While Sook sat in a hut with the shaman, talking and bartering for herbs, Lillie Mae tried her best to attract Teshu's attention. Eventually her persistence wore down his haughty reserve, and the two of them became friends. From the first there was a great deal of passion between the two, although it was several years before they actually became lovers.

Lillie Mae was soon to learn that Teshu was regarded in his own tribe as an aristocrat, whose ancestors included several important chiefs. His great-great-grandfather was William Weatherford, the son of an Indian princess and a Scotch trader, who won an enduring reputation in his tribe as a horseman, athlete, orator, and leader. He established a large plantation on the banks of the Alabama River and spoke the English language with as much eloquence as any white man. In spite of his white genes, Weatherford feared the dangers of further white encroachment on the Creek land. Finally, he raised a great force against the whites, went on the warpath, and fought numerous battles. Far more Indians than whites died in the war. In the end, Weatherford, whose exploits in battle had earned him the Indian name of Red Eagle, negotiated a settlement with General

Andrew Jackson. Weatherford returned to his plantation, where he died in 1824.

Teshu's mother was a Creek princess who intensely disliked all whites. Lillie Mae took me to meet her once. She must have been close to fifty, but she appeared as graceful as the deer in the forest. Teshu's father sat on the tribal council.

None of this, of course, carried any weight in the white communities beyond the reservation. Teshu was simply more grist for the gossip mills.

"He's part French, you know. His father was related to a French missionary. He's got a gait just like a Jesuit priest!"

"I bet his mother was an Osage. That means his maternal grandfather was a rattlesnake!"

"Damn good-looking Indian. But what the hell—an Indian is just one cut above a nigger. Only more dangerous."

And so it went. The pair fell in love and began to see each other on a regular basis but always secretly. Lillie Mae never wanted it known publicly that she was seeing an Indian.

Teshu warned Lillie Mae that their love would never survive the animosities between their two peoples and told her the story of Leopold Lanair and Winona, a Creek maiden, to prove his point. A century before, Prophet François, a Creek chief with French and Scots blood, raised an independent war against the whites stationed at Fort Clairborne. His camp was located on Nannahubba Island at the junction of the Alabama and Tombigbee rivers. One day his warriors captured a white soldier named Leopold Lanair and brought him back to François's camp, tied him to a great tree, and told him to prepare for death at dawn the next day. Guards were posted to keep a careful watch over him through the night. But another watched, too—the beautiful Winona, François's daughter and a princess in her tribe. She felt great sympathy for the handsome white soldier and determined to free him. In the early morning she slipped past the guards and with a knife cut his bonds. Then she led

Leopold to the river's edge where she had hidden a canoe in the bushes. The soldier lingered to drink in her beauty and declare his love. The two exchanged vows before he pushed away in his canoe.

The two met secretly in the forest after that. Leopold feared to disclose his liaison with the Indian princess to his fellow soldiers at Fort Clairborne, and Winona feared the wrath of her father. One evening as they met and embraced, they heard the sound of a twig snapping. Suddenly, the couple found themselves surrounded by François and twelve of his warriors. The chief ordered the warriors to slay Leopold but spare his daughter. The soldier seized his rifle and with a single shot killed the Creek chief. With rifle butt and knife he fought against the other Indians, who forced him to the edge of a high precipice overlooking the river. His foes thought they had him, but in an instant Leopold seized Winona in his arms and leaped off the cliff to the river below. There in a watery grave, side by side, sleep the ill-fated lovers of Creek Indian legend. Teshu often took Lillie Mae to the same high bluff where tradition insisted the couple had leaped to their deaths.

Teshu became the center of all of Lillie Mae's fantasies throughout the summers of 1921 and 1922. She loved to think of him as a sort of Corsican bandit. (Lillie Mae had read Lord Byron's *Childe Harold's Pilgrimage* in school.) When she was with Teshu, all her disdainful, contemptuous arrogance disappeared. To him she was always submissive, yielding, loving, and simple. Teshu, in turn, fell equally in love with this sooty-eyed woman with her cool ways and skin as pale as cream.

Like Leopold and Winona before them, Teshu and Lillie Mae met secretly in the forest near his reservation. She would borrow Jenny's car and drive over to Clairborne to rendezvous with Teshu as often as she could. On many of these trips she asked me along. I was to be their cover. As long as I was there, other people would assume everything between the two of them was innocent. After a while they simply forgot about me. They would talk and act as though I were not even there.

Teshu would declare his love for Lillie Mae with great eloquence. I remember one evening when the three of us were down by the Alabama River at the old landing where sternwheelers once tied up to collect bales of cotton. Fireflies whirled in burning circles above the fingers of fog starting to come off the dark surface of the river. I retreated to the shadows nearby to give them a little more privacy, even though my presence never seemed to disturb them in the slightest.

"Do you love me, Teshu?" Lillie Mae asked.

"Sometimes I am afraid to love you," he answered. "I have seen how you flaunt yourself without shame around other men. I do not think you could be happy with one man."

"Do you love me?" she asked again.

The two of them stood very close.

"I do love you," Teshu finally admitted. "I do love you. I cannot get rid of the thought of you. You are in my very blood. The very touch of your hand on mine . . ."

And then they kissed, gently and innocently.

There were many times when I sensed anger and resentment swelling in Teshu. He and Lillie Mae were separated by barriers more impossible than any confronting Romeo and Juliet. They came from two different races, each suspicious of the other, and lived in a world where loving the wrong race was the one unforgivable sin. Teshu knew Lillie Mae well enough to know that as much as she loved him, she would never make that commitment public. She could flout the moral codes of her society only so much. In her heart, he understood, she was utterly conventional and much too selfish to make the sacrifices such a love demanded.

I was the only family member to know of Lillie Mae's love for Teshu. But our two Negro servants, Corrie and Little Bit, learned of it and disapproved. Little Bit, part Indian herself, vehemently opposed Lillie Mae's attachment to Teshu. The three of us talked about it constantly.

"Dat Lillie Mae is always gwine be trouble fer a man. Dat's de Gawd's truf!" Little Bit would advise us. "If dat Lillie Mae keeps it up, she'll spread dose legs fer dat Indian 'fore she is through. She an' Teshu are like wisteria growin' round a tree. Dey never will be unwound."

Little Bit's warning was prophetic. Lillie Mae and Teshu kept their romance innocent at first, but after her marriage to Arch Persons, Lillie Mae took Teshu as her lover and saw him each time she returned to Monroeville, right up to the time of her suicide.

• CHAPTER THREE •

Arch Persons

THE SUMMER OF 1923 began with an untimely hot spell in June that wilted the japonicas, azaleas, and daffodils in Jenny's backyard and put us all on edge. Not even the thick walls of Jenny's big house were protection against that summer's sticky heat which daily became more oppressive. I recall that at the time I thought of us as living on the edge of a volcano whose rumblings became more violent each day. Lillie Mae was home. She was restless, angry, frustrated, and in a constant bad temper. I knew that before the summer was over something would have to give. I was right. For that summer of 1923 was a fateful time in all our lives. It brought changes that profoundly affected the future of each and every one of us who lived under Jenny's roof.

Lillie Mae was back in Monroeville from the Alabama State Teachers College in Troy. She had insisted that Jenny send her there and then had returned home after completing less than half the semester. Lillie Mae refused to go back. She hated the school, not for the quality of the education it offered but because of its students. As far as Lillie Mae was concerned, Alabama State Teachers College was full of riffraff, and she would have no more of it.

"That's the tackiest school I have ever been to," she told Jenny contemptuously. "Nobody, but nobody goes there."

"You picked it, young lady," Jenny replied, fretful at losing a half year's tuition because of Lillie Mae's fickleness.

71

"I don't give a damn. I will not go back there. I want to go to school in New Orleans. Now *that's* a city that has something to offer."

"New Orleans!" Jenny screamed at her in desperation. "Where in the world would I get the money to send you gallivanting off to New Orleans?"

"Where would you get the money?" Lillie Mae said, cool as could be. "Why, you could use some of that money you stole from us when Popper and Mama died, that's where!" Lillie Mae always believed that when our father died, he left behind a considerable sum of money that Jenny had appropriated. She insisted that Jenny had profited from his death. I doubt it. Anyway, Jenny had given us children a home and never denied any of us anything we wanted. But Lillie Mae early learned exactly where to stick a knife into a person to make it hurt the most.

Jenny's eyes snapped and flashed as she looked at Lillie Mae. "You ungrateful bitch," she shouted. "You make me so mad I could spit!" Instead Jenny picked up a broom that Corrie had left in the parlor and threatened Lillie Mae with it.

"As sure as Monday comes after Sunday, Jenny, you are no better than a damn cotton-patch slut."

Suddenly, Corrie stepped into the parlor. She always seemed to know just the right moment to come into a scene.

"Both youse ladies shut yer moufs 'cause dey has got too big fer yore faces. I'se got a good mind to leave fer once and all. Youse is both scrappin' like alley cats in heat. Dat's de pure truf iffen I ever tol' it."

Before another dawn Lillie Mae would have her head buried deep in Corrie's ample bosom, crying her heart out and telling her how unhappy she was. Corrie would kiss and caress her silky hair and vow to protect her "Peach Blossom." (Peach Blossom was Corrie's pet name for Lillie Mae when she pleased her. When she didn't, Lillie Mae was that "Whore of Babylon.")

Lillie Mae became more desperate with the passing of each

day. She *had* to get out of Monroeville and to New Orleans, no matter what. Life in Jenny's home was too confining. She longed for the excitement of the big city—for a world of money and class, of fast men, fast cars, and expensive restaurants.

Suddenly in the early part of that summer of 1923, Lillie Mae's ticket to that fantasy world appeared in Monroeville, riding in a fancy chauffeur-driven black Packard and sporting one of the most prominent names in the entire state of Alabama. He was Archulus Persons. Arch for short. True, he was not that much to look at, about as far from movie-star good looks as you could get with his thick-lensed glasses. But his family name meant a great deal. His father had been a prominent chemistry professor at the University of Alabama in Tuscaloosa and had once been asked to Washington to confer with President Theodore Roosevelt on some matter. His grandfather had been a governor of Alabama. His mother was a Knox, from one of the wealthiest families in the entire state and highly influential in government and business circles.

Arch was a good friend of the Henderson boys, who lived on a big plantation outside Monroeville where their parents raised some of the finest Thoroughbred horses in the state. They had been fraternity brothers at Washington and Lee University in Lexington, Virginia. Arch would visit them often during the summers. None of them had taken up any serious work since they had finished their studies. Rather they lived off their families' money and led rather wild lives.

Lillie Mae and Arch had seen each other at a distance, first in Troy when she was a student there and later in Monroeville, but as yet there had been no formal introduction. But both were interested in the other—Arch in Lillie Mae for her good looks, and Lillie Mae in Arch for the money and social prestige that his name represented.

"You can't miss that Arch Persons in Troy because he is always riding around high and mighty in the backseat of his chauffeur-driven black Packard," Lillie Mae told me. (Later she learned that Arch's car with its uniformed black chauffeur belonged to his grandmother, Mrs. Knox.) "And he always wears the most god-awful cream-colored panama hat, which he tilts at a crazy angle on the back of his head. But it does make him look like a bit of a rake. And he loves to wear candy-cane-striped silk shirts with white linen suits that have 'MONEY' written all over them."

Lillie Mae asked around, and the more she learned about Arch Persons the more impressed she became. He had been born on September 1, 1897, in Montgomery and had graduated from the prestigious Gulf Coast Military Academy in Gulfport, Mississippi. He had worked as a secretary to the superintendent of the Alabama Power Company plant at Gorgas. A glowing recommendation from the president of the power company had netted him a place at the Washington and Lee University law school, from which he graduated with honors in 1921. Arch never did much with law. He practiced for a short time and then was disbarred for unethical behavior in a divorce case. His two brothers, William Samford and John Knox, made good early marriages and quickly established themselves in business. Arch, on the other hand, was content to tread water for several years and simply enjoy the good times that the more permissive twenties had ushered in. He quickly picked up a reputation as the family's black sheep. His mother provided him with a comfortable allowance, but she was clearly unhappy with his lack of serious ambition.

Lillie Mae and Arch met by chance one afternoon in Monroeville when Arch was in town visiting the Henderson boys for the long Fourth of July weekend. Lillie Mae ran into the three of them as she came out of Monroe Drugs. Before anyone could introduce them properly, Lillie Mae stepped up to Arch and said, "You're Arch Persons, aren't you? I've heard all about you. You're a smooth article. Your family has money that you don't hesitate to spend, you move in the best social circles, run everything your own way, and have very little to do with work."

Arch was completely taken aback. This was hardly complimentary. (Lillie Mae always knew when an unorthodox approach with men would work.) One of his chief reasons for coming to Monroeville, however, was to meet Lillie Mae. He had told several people that he thought she was the most beautiful woman he had ever seen.

Lillie Mae studied Arch Persons carefully as they made small talk. He was a mild-mannered, soft-spoken man with thick glasses that distorted his eyes grotesquely, but that did not matter. Arch was going to be her ticket out of Monroeville, and she was much too impressed by Arch's family connections and the big Packard touring car to worry about his lack of good looks. Money and class always meant a great deal to her. Well, Arch had the class but not the money, and his family was not about to give him any, either; however, Lillie Mae would not find this out until after their marriage. Arch was always a bit of a flim-flam artist, and he pulled a fast one on Lillie Mae.

Arch wanted to know if he could see her.

"I'll be home tomorrow afternoon if you want to come a-calling," Lillie Mae said in her best flirtatious manner. Arch promised to be there.

Sure enough, that next afternoon as Lillie Mae and I sat rocking on our front porch, what should come down the street but Arch's black Packard with his chauffeur at the wheel. (Arch was much too blind ever to drive; Truman inherited his bad eyesight from his father.) With him were Hamp and Albert Henderson, who had always been as wild as ingrowing hairs. Lillie Mae tried to appear unconcerned, but she had dressed up so that she looked a vision of pure delight.

Jenny had found an excuse to stay home from the store that day after Lillie Mae had bragged at the dinner table the previous evening that she had a date with *the* Arch Persons. Jenny, too, had heard all about Arch. "Now, don't you go getting mixed up with that man, young lady," she had warned Lillie Mae. "He's a scoundrel and a disgrace to the Persons family." Of course, words like that to Lillie Mae made about as much sense as waving a red tablecloth in front of an angry bull. But Jenny was never one to hold her tongue.

The Packard stopped in front. Arch stepped out and walked up to the porch. "Good afternoon, Miss Lillie Mae," he said, bowing and flourishing his panama hat. He was a smoothie, all right, no doubt of that. He was stylishly dressed, too. Lillie Mae's eyes checked him over from head to heel as if she were adding up the cost of each of his wardrobe items. You could tell she was impressed. Then we saw he had been drinking and was a little unsteady on his feet.

If it had been just Arch, things might have worked out with no problems at that first meeting. But Hamp and Albert were along. The pair had drunk just enough straight corn liquor to make them noisy and boisterous. Both had known Jenny since they were big enough to come into town, and neither particularly liked her. They were in a frame of mind to raise a little hell. Things began to get out of hand almost immediately.

Bud, hearing the commotion, came onto the front porch. "What in tarnation is going on here?" he demanded. Albert was beating out a tattoo on the Packard's roof and reaching in to press the horn. Hamp staggered out of the car and tried to approach the porch. He was chewing on a toothpick. "Miss Lillie Mae, wouldn't you like to come on a picnic to Hatter's Mill Pond with us this afternoon?" he asked, and then stumbled and fell on the grass.

The old Negro driving Arch's car was getting worried. He started pleading, "White folks . . . white folks" over and over again.

Poor Arch. He was not drunk enough to be blind to the fact that his friends were ruining his chances with Lillie Mae.

Jenny came out on the porch to survey the scene. "Lillie Mae and Tiny," she shouted to us, "you two go straight inside this minute. And you, Arch Persons, get the hell away from my house. Don't you ever come here again in this condition."

We went into the living room and hid behind the drapes where we could watch and hear everything out front.

Hamp and Albert were telling Arch to get back to the car. They claimed their afternoon was ruined and were trying to talk him into a trip to Rooktown. "Well, boys," Albert said, "poon-tang is what we are after, and we can get plenty of that in Rooktown."

Arch tried to beg off, but he lacked the courage to stand up to Hamp and Albert. They all piled into Arch's Packard and drove off. In less than thirty minutes they were back.

The three of them walked straight up to the front porch and knocked on the screen door. Lillie Mae burst out and hit Arch so hard on the side of his head that his glasses flew off and landed among the japonica bushes in the yard.

Lillie Mae was furious. She scratched and screamed. "Get away from me," she shouted. "Whew! You smell funky. Smell just like a nigger. . . . Get away from me, you damn nigger lover."

"Lillie," Arch said pitifully.

"Damn you, don't call me Lillie," Lillie Mae screamed.

"What's wrong? That's your name, isn't it?"

"No, it's Lillie *Mae*. Lillie is a nigger name, but since you are a nigger lover it would probably suit you just fine to give me a nigger's name."

Just then Corrie came out. "Lillie Mae, you shut yore mouf. Jes 'cause us is black you ain't got no call to call us niggers. We is humans, too. Gal, I may be black on de outside, but you is shore black on de insides."

"Shut your black mouth, Corrie! Do you hear me?"

"I hears you all right. An' don't you gets uppity with me, 'cause I knows what an' don't you fergit dat, Lillie Mae."

"What the hell do you mean?" Lillie Mae demanded.

But she knew exactly what Corrie meant—her crush on Teshu. That was the last thing she wanted anyone to know. So Lillie Mae turned back to Arch, who was out in the front yard on his hands and knees feeling around in the grass for his glasses.

Lillie Mae jumped off the porch and said sweetly, "I'll help you find them, Arch."

"Thank you, Lillie Mae," Arch said, grateful for the assistance. Without his glasses he was almost blind.

"Here they are," Lillie Mae called.

"Thank you, Lillie Mae," Arch said.

"Here. Give me your hand. Feel them now?" Lillie Mae asked in a patronizing voice.

"Yes, thank God."

Before Arch could grasp them securely, Lillie Mae took the heel of her shoe and ground the lenses into splinters, then picked up the frame and snapped it like a dry twig.

Arch was practically in tears, more over the disastrous first date with Lillie Mae than the loss of his glasses. He rode off in his car almost immediately. Lillie Mae, however, knew he would be back. She also knew she would see him again. He still represented her escape from Monroeville.

"I kin feel Mr. Arch got a hankering after you," Corrie told Lillie Mae a few weeks later after Arch had called several more times at the big house. She had her suspicions that the two would be getting married. It was obvious that Arch was completely taken with Lillie Mae. "He's as techy as a mule in fly time, chile. But I don' want you marryin' no floozy-chasin' man, honey. He ain't gwine make you happy."

But Lillie Mae was in no mood to take any advice from anyone on her affairs of the heart.

Theirs was a whirlwind courtship punctuated by moments of absurd comedy that might have been scripted by Mack Sennett. One Monday afternoon Arch, Hamp, and Albert rode into town from the big Henderson plantation on the high-spirited horses they were famous for. All three had been drinking heavily of bootleg corn whiskey. They came galloping into town, riding up and down on the sidewalks, chasing people into the streets, and generally making themselves obnoxious. Suddenly, Hamp and Arch rode their horses smack into the drugstore just to one side of Jenny's store. This was her property. And she was over there within two minutes.

Jenny was furious. The first thing she did was to grab at Arch as he rode his horse around in circles on the tile floor and drag him off his saddle. At that point Hamp figured he had best dismount and try to get his horse back out the front door and onto the street. Jenny was screaming at the top of her lungs and swatting at horses and riders alike with a long wooden walking stick she had grabbed on her way over. In the excitement the two horses lost control and dropped bucket-size piles of turds all over the white tile floor.

God, you would not believe the commotion. You have to remember that the marble-topped tables and stools at the fountain were full of schoolkids sipping milkshakes and Cokes. All the young people loved it! What excitement! The sidewalk outside was crowded with townspeople.

Jenny finally managed to get the horses out of the drugstore. "Damn you two to hell for the problems you've made today!" she shouted to Arch and Hamp. "You are going to burn in hell if there is any justice in this world!" (She was half right about that. A few years later Hamp Henderson fell into a drunken stupor in an old house and burned himself to death while trying to light a cigarette.)

Jenny called one of the schoolkids over. "Go around to the back of my store and get old John White to come here," she told the youngster. John was close to ninety years old. Jenny kept him around because he had once worked for my father. He wasn't much good anymore, but Jenny called on him for the odd job and gave him enough money every month to buy the necessities of life.

John slowly shuffled into view. He was a short, stubby Negro. He took one look inside the drugstore at the floor. "Jes look at dat," he said. "It make a body want to puke."

"John, never you mind. Just clean this mess up."

"Yes'm."

It took a while, but John finally had the floor as white as before.

Later, after the drugstore was cleaned up and aired out, people started returning to its dim coolness. A tall, thin boy with straight yellow hair that fell forward into a sort of curl on his forehead and a short girl with dark brown hair combed away from her face sat down at a table and ordered two Cokes.

They didn't talk much. The girl slowly sucked the cola through a straw and from time to time lifted the glass to her mouth and let bits of crushed ice drop onto her tongue.

She smiled at him. You could see his one hand under the table slowly reach for her knee and then hastily pull away at the last moment.

This had been a strange, hot July. The temperature hit ninety-five degrees, and just stayed there. This was the summer that Lillie Mae married Arch Persons.

Lillie Mae at first had wanted a simple wedding. But Jenny

would have nothing of that. The Faulks would marry off Lillie Mae in grand style. Jenny, after all, had her image to uphold.

The day of the wedding came, August 23, 1923. The big house awoke earlier than usual. The servants, Corrie, Little Bit, and Sem, who helped out on special occasions, were doing a hundred tasks before any of us were awake. Great displays of flowers continued to arrive throughout the morning from florists in Mobile.

A half-dozen workmen had come the day before and erected striped pink awnings with lots of small iron tables in the backyard. (In those days we never referred to a "yard" as a "lawn.")

Jenny had spent a small fortune on Lillie Mae's bridal gown. She had even sent to St. Louis for a set of white satin undergarments. Each piece had Lillie Mae's name embroidered on it.

Lillie Mae's girl friends had come from Troy and New Orleans and stayed at Jenny's house. Breakfast was served to the girls in their bedrooms. Everywhere there was confusion and noise, running and dressing.

And the talk was of men, men, and men. "Is it really true that men with big noses have big peckers, that men with small turned-up noses are built like boys, and that men with long thin noses are the best because their peckers are real long?"

"Did you see that thing between that nigger Sem's legs the other day as he lay sleeping under the big oak tree out back? Bong! Bong!"

The talk shifted to the days when they would all get married. Would they get twelve bridesmaids, two orchestras, sixteen ushers, and thousands of wedding presents?

Arch had given Lillie Mae an engagement ring with a diamond that was on the small side. Lillie Mae showed it to her bridesmaids and told them, "He won't get away with this after we are married. I am sick and tired of people holding my hand and saying, 'How sweet.'"

"My God," somebody yelled out. "Who sent these awful blue candlesticks?"

"Earmark them for Corrie," Lillie Mae hollered back.

"Say, Lillie Mae," one of her friends confided, "do you know that Arch hasn't a hair on his body? It's like baby skin. I know. I saw him the other day lying out at Hatters's Mill Pond with just a towel around him. Personally, I like a man with some hair on his body."

Lillie Mae knew that, and it bothered her, too. She also felt a shiver of uncontrollable disgust sometimes at the things Arch said and the way he said them. Nothing upset her more than when he pleaded with her, saying, "Please love me. Nobody will love you like I do. Please love me."

But Lillie Mae resolved to make the best of it because at the moment Archulus Persons was what she wanted, and she was not one to look back. The night before the wedding, on an impulse, I walked with Corrie out into the backyard. We found Lillie Mae leaning against a magnolia tree. I knew she would be there.

"Lillie Mae," Corrie said, "don' let yore mine rest on dat Injin."

Lillie Mae suddenly burst into tears and wept uncontrollably. We could tell that she was all torn up inside.

"Lillie Mae," Corrie insisted, "youse got to fergit dat Injin. It's yore time to marry. Ain't healthy for a gal to put off marryin' once she's reached her bloomin' time. Behave you'self an' don't turn over any stones, 'cause all yo is gwinter find is worms."

That was Corrie's way of saying, "Lillie Mae, be happy!"

Lillie Mae did pull herself together. She didn't let anyone else see how she felt inside.

Jenny gave a huge dinner for the entire wedding party, and there were luncheons and teas all over town. Lillie Mae was the bride but Jenny, as usual, was the queen of the show. She personally greeted all the guests. She had just turned fifty, but you could never have guessed her age from the way she looked that day. She wore a pink chiffon dress. On her fingers she had diamond rings that flashed in the sunlight. Around her neck hung a gold chain studded with rubies and diamonds. Jenny had reached that age when she did not have to depend on her sex to achieve her objectives. Yet she never for a moment neglected the advantage of her femininity. Men smiled at her cordially. They respected and liked her as a business figure, but they also found her pleasing as a woman. Jenny, in turn, liked to receive their smiles, and she never, never underestimated the tonic of masculine admiration. To maintain it, she would mingle the flattery of the Southern belle with the intuition of maturity, while recognizing also the unfailing value of remembering the likes and dislikes of each man she met. Once she discovered that a man enjoyed a certain drink, he had it that way each time he came to visit her. If he preferred a certain chair, he always got it. His interests and hobbies seemed almost to be her interests and hobbies when he brought them into the conversation.

Of Arch's family only his mother and younger brother, John, came to Monroeville for his wedding. (I was later engaged to John, but that didn't last very long. I couldn't stand the man.) Arch's father was dead, and his mother had remarried. His stepfather decided to remain in Troy. The Persons family was always on the cool side, not warm like the Faulks. After the marriage Arch and Lillie Mae rarely visited his family. Both preferred the Faulk household in Monroeville. After Truman was born, Arch's family took no interest in him either—not until years later, after he had become famous. Then, of course, they couldn't say enough nice things about him. But this is running ahead of my story.

After the wedding Arch took Lillie Mae on a honeymoon trip to New York City, then to Pensacola, Florida, and finally to New Orleans. We put them on the train, the *Crescent Limited*, that passed through Flomaton, Alabama, about thirty miles from

Monroeville, every midnight. The train did not stop at Flomaton unless there was a passenger, and then you had to wait
outside on the platform and be quick about getting on.

I do not like to think about Flomaton, Alabama. Another
time many years later I met Lillie Mae in Monroeville after she
had married Joe Capote. Joe had just lost his job and was under
indictment for embezzlement. She had come home, grasping for
something—I don't know what. The last time I saw Lillie Mae
alive she was sitting on her suitcase in the tiny Flomaton station
waiting for the midnight train to carry her back to New York
and death.

After the honeymoon Arch and Lillie Mae settled in New
Orleans. For a while Lillie Mae had realized her dream. They
lived in one of the nicest residential hotels. Arch pampered her
with moonlight boat rides on the Mississippi River, top-name
restaurants, and dancing in nightclubs until the sun came up.
Lillie Mae had clothes from Bergdorf Goodman, DePinna's, and
other fine New York stores. I remember her telling me how
much she loved Andrew Geller shoes. She had a huge selection
of shoes; I think she had a pair dyed to match every summer
dress in her closet. Pink, blue, red, lavender shoes—with straps
that wrapped around her ankles.

Arch did not have a job yet. At the time of his marriage he
had received a considerable sum of money from his mother—
she had always spoiled him that way—and an older brother had
given him a handsome sum as a wedding present. So Arch and
Lillie Mae lived high on the hog in New Orleans for a while.
But time and money were quickly running out, and Arch's
mother was not about to support her son's frivolous life-style
indefinitely.

Finally they frittered away all of Arch's money. Arch came
to Jenny and showed her Lillie Mae's diamond engagement ring
and asked if she would lend him $500 against it (far more than it

was worth). She did. But Arch never repaid the loan, and so Lillie Mae never got her ring back.

By the end of the year Arch had moved them into a cheaper hotel. They stopped eating at fancy restaurants and took to eating more often in their room. Arch loved cans of Heinz's pork and beans and ate them by the case. That used to drive Lillie Mae crazy.

Finally, in January of 1924, Arch got his first real job. He was hired as an assistant purser with the Streckfus Steamship Company in New Orleans, earning $450 a month. Streckfus owned several old-fashioned riverboats, wood-burning paddle wheels with two high smokestacks that were straight out of an earlier era of Mississippi River travel. They ran up the river on excursions as far north as St. Louis. Arch worked on a ship called the *Capitol* that operated on the run between New Orleans and St. Louis. The ship carried some cargo, but basically it was a pleasure boat. Old man Streckfus figured a well-educated young man from a prominent Southern family would be a definite asset on the staff of this particular ship, which often featured a well-known New Orleans band. Arch loved his job and held it for many years. (In 1928 when he took his four-year-old son, Truman, on one of the cruises, Louis Armstrong and his band were playing on board. Truman tap-danced while Satchmo shouted encouragement. That trip provided Truman with one of his favorite stories.)

Arch spent his time between trips ashore with Lillie Mae in their hotel, but Lillie Mae was unhappy with her life in New Orleans. She was tired of hotel rooms and restaurant meals, and she was lonely. Lillie Mae had made few friends, male or female, in New Orleans. She and Arch did not have the kind of money she needed to break into the only sort of society that really interested her.

Lillie Mae soon became homesick for Monroeville, especially the big Sunday dinners at Jenny's house. She and Arch would arrive on Saturday evening, stay for Sunday dinner, and then head back to New Orleans about 3:00 P.M.

Lillie Mae would always tell Jenny, "I'm hungry for some good old-fashioned Southern home cooking." At that time Arch would take her evenings to any cafeteria near their hotel.

Our dining-room table at Jenny's seated ten comfortably. Whatever children there were sat at smaller tables placed to one side, each of which was set with linen, silver, and food exactly like the big table. It has always been a Southern custom to invite over for Sunday dinner those who were new in town, or had a sickness in the family, or had just had a death. So we never knew who might be there.

Our Sunday dinners never varied. We had steak with brown gravy, fresh yellow corn on the cob with lots of melted butter, and fresh yellow squash with onions. There were platters of tomatoes when in season, cucumbers, hot peppers, bell peppers, and a big bowl of boiled okra. When we were young, it was fun to hold our heads back and let the moist, slimy okra slide down our throats. All Southern kids got whacked for doing this disgusting thing at the dinner table, and we Faulk kids (and later Truman) were certainly no exception. Little Bit would bring in big plates of high buttermilk biscuits and steaming "lace corn pone." For dessert we had freshly baked blackberry cobbler buried beneath mounds of whipped cream, or pound cake with a crusty top, or the best pecan pie in the state (or so Bud used to tell Little Bit).

And sometimes ice cream. Often during the summer months we would gather in the backyard and make fresh ice cream. Peach, strawberry, and blackberry were our favorite flavors. We would fill the hand-operated freezer with freshly sliced fruit, thick cream, sugar, custard, and whatever and then pack in the ice. The children would have the honor of pouring the rock salt around the edge and slowly turning the handle, being careful not to let the salt get on top. Finally, after what seemed like hours, the ice cream would harden and be ready to serve.

Oddly enough, after Lillie Mae had married and moved to New Orleans, she began to miss Monroeville. Not that she would have been happy had she moved back. Lillie Mae was born to be restless, unhappy with what she had, and convinced that life would be better elsewhere or with a different man. She looked for happiness all her life and never really found it except for short periods.

Lillie Mae began to take out her frustrations on Arch. He seemed rather weak compared to her, too vacillating and passive to resist her. He became in the end something like a house pet for her. I think that almost from the day they were married "petticoat rule" was the name of their game. Lillie Mae progressively usurped Arch's masculine sphere. She often held him up to ridicule and was quick to humiliate him when the opportunity presented itself. And matters were not helped by the obvious fact that they were mismatched sexually. Arch was low-keyed. Sex was never an important matter to him. He could take it or leave it. Lillie Mae, on the other hand, was deeply passionate with a sex drive that she could not always control. Poor Arch. From the first he was overwhelmed by the intensity of his wife's sexual passion and simply could not cope with it.

Lillie Mae came back to Monroeville more and more. She was sad and didn't appear to notice things around her much. Early one morning the two of us were sitting on the back steps. Lillie Mae started talking in a hesitating, uncertain way about her life with Arch in New Orleans. I could sense a fear, some sort of urgent conflict waiting to come out. She drew a deep breath and threw back her head. Her words when they came out were slurred.

"Tiny, I am caught. I am pregnant."

I nodded, not knowing what to say.

Lillie Mae drew in her breath as though she was going to cry. But she didn't.

I felt the tears coming into my own eyes. I could not bear to see my sister so worn and beaten.

"Oh, sweet Jesus. Why did this have to happen to me?"

I tried to reassure her. "Now, Lillie Mae, things will work out," I said.

"How the hell are we going to pay the hospital bill, pray tell?" she said in an agonized whisper.

"Now, Lillie Mae, don't you worry . . . don't you worry now. We will all help you out. Besides, you should be happy at having a baby."

"I should be happy? Happy? Oh, God, I won't be able to stand the sight of my stomach all stuck out. And besides, I hate Arch Persons. We are half starving to death. I have almost no spending money. I wish it wasn't so, but that's the way it is. I don't want his baby."

There was a long pause.

"I could get an operation, I suppose, if I could get the money. I know a doctor in New Orleans . . ."

"God, Lillie Mae, if you do anything crazy like that, I'll tell Jenny, I swear I will."

"Jenny, hell, she doesn't care one bit," Lillie Mae said in near despair. "She didn't want me to marry Arch in the first place. For once she was right. I wish I had listened to her. But now I just don't want to hear her jawing me, saying, 'I told you so.' I couldn't stand that."

She let her breath hiss out between her teeth.

"I am all alone. I've got no one."

"Damn you, Lillie Mae," I said, "that's not true. You have all of us. Tell Jenny before she goes off to the store. She will stand by you.

"*Jenny*," I called out at the top of my lungs before Lillie Mae could answer. "*Jenny!*" Another frantic call for help.

Suddenly Corrie appeared. She had heard me call and knew that tone of voice meant some sort of trouble. Jenny, too, must have realized that something out of the ordinary was at stake because she came out quietly and asked what the problem was.

"Jenny, I have gone and done it. I am pregnant," Lillie Mae told her.

This was in January of 1924. The first chill of winter was in the air. There had been frost on the grass in the early morning.

Corrie was the first to speak. She sprang up and said, "I'se knowed it, I'se knowed it. De mockin' birds is sassin' one another. Dat's a sure sign."

"Sure sign of what?" Jenny wanted to know.

"Why, Miz Jenny, a sure sign of birthin'. An' iffen I'se livin' I gonna see dat chile is raised in de ways of Gawd."

Little Bit was silently cooking breakfast in the kitchen, but she was taking everything in. Finally she hollered out the window, "I hopes it ain't no boy-chile. It ain't no good to have a boy-chile raised wid a house full o' womenfolk."

Jenny sat there awhile longer. Finally, she spoke. "Well, Lillie Mae, I must admit I am put out. But I promise you that your child will never have to wear gunny-sack clothes during the week and flour-sack clothes on Sunday."

I sat there, thinking to myself, "My God, Jenny, put your arms around Lillie Mae and let her know that you care."

But Jenny never did.

Jenny kept her word. Her sense of loyalty to her family won out over her differences with Lillie Mae. Jenny made certain that she received the best medical care possible throughout her pregnancy. She put Lillie Mae under the care of a doctor in Mobile. Arch insisted that the baby be born in New Orleans where he worked for the Streckfus Steamship Company. Jenny gave in but had to pay all the hospital costs anyway.

Lillie Mae spent most of the later months of her pregnancy in Monroeville where all of us pampered her outrageously. She ate all the fried chicken, grits, fresh mayhaw jelly, and peach ice cream that she could hold. The whole household tried to buck up Lillie Mae's spirits, but she seemed to wither like a night-blooming cactus as the dawn breaks in the desert.

Corrie just about drove everyone crazy with her voodoo. She was afraid that the child would be born during a full moon. "De night of de full moon is de mos' beautiful but also de mos' dangerous," she would say to whoever would listen. "Good an' evil spirits fly fer an' wide. Dead peoples rise up an' walk to de places dey hated an' loved. Ain't no time to birth a chile into de world."

Lillie Mae, too, looked ahead to the birth with dread. Emotionally she was still a child, quite incapable of seeing beyond her own selfish needs. Her imagination worked overtime exaggerating the pain of the birth itself. She dreaded the sleepless nights and feared the damage to her breasts that might come with feeding her infant. She intensely disliked the interruption in her life that motherhood involved. All these fears caused Lillie Mae to look upon Truman, when he finally did arrive, as a terrible nuisance and an unacceptable obstacle that threatened her carefully constructed plans for moving into the Social Register.

Lillie Mae had neither the strength nor the courage to cope with the ordeal of motherhood. She once told me that she blamed Arch for her pregnancy and resented him for it. Lillie Mae felt that he had betrayed her and his love for her. Thus, she turned her pregnancy into resentment against Arch rather than letting it become the joy it should have been. She never forgave either Arch or Truman. After his birth Lillie Mae continued in her own life with as few interruptions as possible. She was never able to devote herself to the needs of her child or to identify herself with his interests as he grew older.

When the time for the birth approached, Jenny took time off from her store to attend to Lillie Mae. She moved the two of them to the elegant Ponce de Leon Hotel in New Orleans to await the start of the labor pains. Jenny did not stay around for the baby to be born. She returned to Monroeville as soon as Lillie Mae entered the hospital.

Truman was born on September 30, 1924. Lillie Mae's anxieties made it a difficult birth. As soon as she could check out of the hospital, Lillie Mae took her baby straight to Monroeville. On the day that he was brought home and placed in her arms, Jenny looked as though she might have owned every stick and stone in the state of Alabama and been willing to chuck them all for the baby Truman. I am certain Jenny had known long before then that the responsibility for raising the child would fall on her shoulders, but she never flinched.

Callie merely looked at the little Truman without saying a word and then went into the parlor to play one of her silvery piano pieces (probably something by Debussy).

Sook was wide-eyed with joy and thrilled beyond words.

When Bud was asked to hold him, he looked down at the sleeping Truman and said, "Hell, no. He looks like a piece of crinkled-up red crepe paper. Let him dry out some."

Jenny insisted on having the family doctor, Dr. Bayles, come in and check out both mother and child. He advised Lillie Mae to nurse the new baby. At Jenny's insistence, she tried it. But not for long. Lillie Mae claimed she could not because Truman would bite her nipples and pinch her breast cruelly between his thumb and forefinger while he suckled.

Corrie, however, knew exactly what was going on. "Lillie Mae ain't gonna let nobody suck on her tits an' git dem all saggin' an' sapped," she told Jenny.

Lillie Mae quickly found herself bored with the responsibilities of motherhood and once again began to grow restless.

"Why don't you just put me in a cage and fix a lock on the door and be done with it?" she shouted one day at Jenny.

The two of them quarreled constantly. At each confrontation Sook would rush to her room and cry so hard that her nose swelled up badly, to the point where she could hardly breathe.

From her bedroom Sook could hear Jenny berating Lillie Mae for neglecting her maternal duties. "My God, girl, you have to get rid of some of your highfalutin ideas and come down to earth. I built what I have out of sweat and guts . . . sweat and guts . . . that's what has held this family together all these years. With a little gumption you could do the same."

But it did no good. Lillie Mae was beyond Jenny's reproaches. She would slap lazily at a mosquito while Jenny yelled at her or twist a lock of her hair. She really didn't give a damn what Jenny thought. She always had a wildness in her that could not be tamed.

I think Truman, the writer, understood this. He put some of Lillie Mae into Holly Golightly in *Breakfast at Tiffany's*. "Never love a wild thing, Mr. Bell," he has her say at one point. "That was Doc's [her first husband] mistake. He was always lugging home wild things. A hawk with a hurt wing. One time it was a full-grown bobcat with a broken leg. But you can't give your heart to a wild thing: the more you do, the stronger they get. Until they're strong enough to run into the woods. Or fly into a tree. Then a taller tree. Then the sky. That's how you'll end up, Mr. Bell. If you let yourself love a wild thing. You end up looking at the sky."

CHAPTER FOUR

Sook

SOOK WAS TRUMAN'S FAVORITE of all of us who lived under the roof of her sister Jenny's big house. She was a constant companion to her young cousin during those years he spent in Monroeville. After Lillie Mae and Arch literally abandoned their infant son with us, it was Sook, more than any other, who had the responsibility for his daily care. The two shared many adventures together in that time. Much later, after Sook died in January of 1946 and after Truman had become famous, he put her at the center of three of his most popular pieces—*The Grass Harp*, *The Thanksgiving Visitor*, and *A Christmas Memory*. Sook's influence on Truman was, thus, profound. But it was not always constructive. With the clear-eyed perception that time brings, I can see now how Sook and Bud each beckoned the young Truman down very different paths to manhood. Sook's influence eventually proved the stronger. But I have often wondered how different things might have been for Truman today had he chosen to walk down Bud's path.

Sook was one of those obscure spinsters who spend their entire lives in limbos created especially for them on the outer fringes of large families. It was as if, years before at her father's death, the family had simply put her in a corner and forgotten about her, the way you do with a floor lamp or a bit of bric-a-brac. She had no social life at all and no clearly defined sphere of responsibility in the household. Her sisters and brother regarded her as a sort of child who had grown older but never up.

Sook (or Nanny, as some of us called her) was like a little shadow in the mainstream of our lives, but she taught us many good things. From her we learned to love and respect nature, to care for helpless and friendless creatures, and to see beauty in things that otherwise went unnoticed.

Sook was a small woman, under five feet tall and weighing less than a hundred pounds, but as bouncy as a coiled steel wire. Many years before she had had all her teeth pulled, but Jenny could never persuade her to keep the "store-bought" dentures in her mouth for long. As a result, her jaws had shrunk, giving her a somewhat ghoulish appearance. For as long as I can remember, Sook wore her white hair cropped close to her head. She was a quiet, gentle woman, always in the background, never demanding and rarely receiving. She was the winsome but homely moss rose who wandered at will, taking care to keep out from underfoot of her sisters and brother.

Sook usually dressed in the same manner at all times. Her dress was a shapeless gingham, preferably blue with small checks, and a white apron with two huge pockets in front which she tied behind in a big bow. She never outwardly showed any affection for the rest of us who lived in Jenny's house, except to Truman, whom she adored. But in her own way she was kind to all of us.

Sook was highly eccentric, but at the time we never thought twice about her little idiosyncrasies. We simply accepted them as normal for her. For instance, Sook was always suspicious of the night air. As a result, she rarely left the house after dusk. Outside, she insisted, lurked the clammy miasma, the deadly swamp fever, and the eternal dampness that could kill a body. For protection she always kept her bedroom windows tightly sealed, no matter how hot and sticky the summer nights might become.

The air in Sook's bedroom was always close and uncomfortable, rank with the smell of stale sweat. Corrie would come in some mornings and over Sook's feeble protests throw open all the windows and doors. "Dis here room stinks!" she would exclaim in disgust. "Yo oughten to sleep shet up in dis hot room, Miz Nanny. Yo might come down with de T.B. Whew! Dis shore stinks!" But such lectures never did Sook any good. As soon as Corrie left the room, Sook would hurriedly close off the bedroom once again.

At the beginning of each day Sook would hold her Bible tightly in her hands against her breasts and ask God to send her a message to guide her through that particular day. If the sun was shining, she would be reluctant to stay inside. Instead she would prefer to poke her way through the tangle of flowers and bushes in our backyard, muttering to herself, "Where is that old cantankerous brood hen, Mizzie? Gone off to the woods somewhere and hidden, that's where! Never mind. When she gets hungry, she'll be back!"

Sook had a talent for mixing colors and sketching. I always thought that if she had been encouraged and perhaps had received some formal training, she might have developed into an artist. Her favorite subjects were butterflies, songbirds, and blooming plants. During the long winter evenings Sook would sit and cut pictures from the stack of magazines the household set aside for her. Some of the pictures she used to decorate the kites she loved to make. Others she would carefully trim, then she painted on their backs a thin solution of flour and water and pasted them on the sides of wastebaskets. Some evenings she and Truman would sort through the stacks of pictures she had saved, discussing how each could be best used. Many of them, Sook insisted, were simply too beautiful to cut. Those were just to keep and look at often.

Over the years Sook had carefully ordered her life around her "hankerings," her name for those activities that completely preoccupied her attention and time at certain months of the year. She posted a list of them on the kitchen wall and followed it faithfully. Whenever we wanted to know what Sook was doing, we could go to that list and read the activity for the month, which never varied from year to year:

> *January and February: cut out pictures.*
> *March: plant bulbs for the spring flowers.*
> *April: make soft soap.*
> *May: collect roots and herbs.*
> *June: make dropsy medicine.*
> *July: bake wedding cakes and give them away.*
> *August and September: canning and preserving.*
> *October: prepare fruitcakes.*
> *November: fix cheese straws for Thanksgiving.*
> *December: prepare Christmas decorations and gifts.*

Sook's bedroom was located just off the kitchen. This was perfect, as her biggest love was cooking and preserving. She filled our pantry to capacity with all sorts of jellies and preserves; she carefully arranged everything according to its color. Sook made our pantry into her own personal art gallery. She had a clear conception of just what colors ought to sit next to each other on the shelves. Her own favorites were the clear, red-amber mayhaw jellies that, she thought, looked best next to the jars of yellow cling peaches, brandied in applejack she had bought from her Indian friend Victorio. The purplish red strawberries, the pear preserves, the pale pink cherries, the dark brown "Turkey" figs—everything found its place on our pantry shelves according to Sook's own color index system, the logic of which the rest of us understood only imperfectly. She and Little Bit, our cook, battled constantly over whether space in the pantry was to be used for preserves or everyday dishes.

Sook's brandied yellow cling peaches were served only on Sunday. Little Bit would open several jars and pour the contents and juice into a large cut-glass bowl, adding some freshly cut springs of mint leaves from our yard. Little Bit always started the preparations for the big Sunday dinner right after breakfast. Church services were over at noon sharp. The custom in our house and throughout Monroeville was to eat the big meal of the day shortly after noon. The servants were then given the rest of Sunday off. Most of the Negro church services were held in the afternoon and early evening.

One Sunday morning we were all dressed for church. Truman, my sister Mary Ida, and I sat on the swing of our front porch to await the arrival of the others. One by one we got up to go to the dining room to get a peach out of the big cut-glass bowl. They were so strong with applejack that we were afraid to eat too many. At first we allowed Truman only one bite, but as the minutes stretched out and Jenny, Bud, and Callie did not show up for the walk to church, the three of us ate more and more of the peaches.

Soon we were all tipsy, laughing and running over the porch. Truman and Mary Ida sat on the swing while I stood behind and pushed them higher and higher, until their feet almost touched the ceiling. The noise got so loud that Little Bit came to the front porch, took one look, and went to fetch Jenny.

We immediately stopped the swing. When we did, Truman fell out like a sack of cornmeal into a dead heap on the floor. He was so drunk he had passed out!

"Miz Jenny! Miz Jenny!" we could hear Little Bit calling frantically. "Y'all come see what Miz Nanny's peaches done to dem chilluns. Jes yo come an' takes a look at my table. Most all dem peaches is et up. Dis is dreadfulsome."

Jenny stormed onto the front porch, followed by Callie, Bud, and Sook. Callie took one look, put her white linen handkerchief to her nose, and disappeared quickly inside. Bud grinned. "I hope you bunch of jackrabbits left something for me," he said good-naturedly. Sook rushed, sobbing, over to the limp Truman, fearful he was dead. Jenny simply laughed and laughed and laughed. After that morning Little Bit made it a point never again to put out the brandied peaches until just before dinner was served.

Our kitchen was immense, probably the largest room in the house. The cast-iron wood-burning stove belonged to Sook, and Sook alone. Jenny had ordered it in St. Louis. There were four cooking eyes, a warmer above for biscuits and bread, a hot-water tank on one side, and a huge baking oven below. It was trimmed in gleaming solid brass. Sook kept a pot of coffee boiling on the stove, day and night. Little Bit liked her coffee with honey. Corrie liked hers with molasses. Sook took hers with lots of sugar.

Little Bit had another stove on the opposite side of the kitchen where she prepared the family meals, and there was a smaller, modern kerosene stove for Callie. She was eternally drinking tea and complaining so much about the taste of the water from the iron kettles that Jenny finally bought her the little kerosene stove just for her to heat her water.

Sook was a sucker for any stray or lost animal or child that came along. Before Truman there was the blind boy who came to live with the Jones family up the street from Jenny's house. Sook felt sorry for him and took him little cakes and batches of cookies that she had baked. One day the boy told her that his biggest regret was that the Jones family had no piano, which he had played before he went blind. So Sook let him play ours, going down every afternoon to walk him up to our house. The boy died not long after coming to Monroeville, and Sook was grief-stricken for months.

Sook was a great influence on the young Truman simply because she included him in most of her activities. Whether it was constructing kites, gathering herbs, hunting pecans for the fruitcakes, making dolls out of grass, or tinting sandpaper for the fireplace matchboxes, Sook and Truman were certain to be seen working contentedly together, oblivious to the rest of the world.

One of their favorite activities was the annual fall preparation of the fruitcakes. (Truman wrote about these experiences at some length in A Christmas Memory.) Sook was a teetotaler herself, but she loved to douse her fruitcakes with good whiskey. Of course, during Prohibition she had to get moonshine corn whiskey. Sook bought hers from Victorio, a rather mean-tempered Indian who lived in a shack on the banks of the Little River about eight miles from Monroeville. He ran a fish camp and, some people insisted, a whorehouse. We never knew for certain about the latter. He was a huge, gap-toothed man with a sallow complexion. Victorio was ugly, and he was tough. (Truman put him in A Christmas Memory as Mr. Haha Jones.)

Victorio claimed to be a full-blooded Apache who had come to Little River from New Mexico. He told us he was named for the famous Apache guerrilla fighter Victorio, who went on the warpath against the whites in the 1880s and was finally killed in a fight with Mexican troops a few years later.

Victorio's whiskey must have been good because lots of people in the county drank it. He was his own best customer and stayed drunk most of the time. Sook was an old customer from way back, always buying the whiskey for her fruitcakes from "Chief Victorio," as she insisted upon calling him.

"Chief Victorio, it is not good for you to drink so much of your whiskey," Sook once cautioned him.

"The white man crazy over tobacco, the Indian crazy over whiskey" was his answer.

Victorio's fish camp/whorehouse was a bad place, all right. Many unpleasant things had happened there—fights, knifings, beatings, and even an occasional shooting. One time Victorio lost his patience with a rowdy customer and knocked him into a roaring fire. Or so the stories insisted. But his camp was always quiet when we were there.

When the rest of us accompanied Sook on one of her whiskey-buying expeditions, it was, we thought, an adventure fraught with terrible dangers. We always approached Victorio's camp with extreme caution, never knowing what awful atrocities might happen while we were there. Sook, on the other hand, never had the slightest hesitation. Victorio showed great tenderness and regard for Sook and her fruitcakes, and he always gave her a friendly welcome.

"Please, Chief Victorio," Sook would say, after they had made small talk for several minutes, "we would like two quarts of your best whiskey."

Each October Sook would offer to pay him for his whiskey, but Victorio would always refuse. "Very well, Chief Victorio," Sook would promise, "I will bring you two of my fruitcakes." She would, too. The big Indian loved her fruitcakes. He would pull up a crate and a bottle of his moonshine whiskey and eat big chunks of the cake while slugging away at his bottle.

Everybody knew that Victorio had a wife, but none of us had ever seen her. Truman had read somewhere that among the Apaches it was customary to disfigure an erring wife by cutting off her nose. We wondered—did Victorio keep his wife hidden because he had amputated her nose in a fit of drunken jealousy? We never found out.

Sook was always making something. Every April it was soft soap, which she made using an old recipe that went back to the early days of deprivation on the Faulk Plantation during Reconstruction. Throughout the rest of the year she would collect all the ashes from the oak logs we burned in our fireplaces and put them in a big iron pot out back. When April came around, Sook would get a fire roaring, boil water in another large cast-iron black pot, and pour it over the ashes in the second pot to make a powerful solution of potash. This she boiled until it was a thick mixture, strong enough to take the skin off your hand had you been foolish enough to dip it into the unsightly solution. Then she would add hog cuts from the little farm that Bud and his black sharecropper, Sylvester, worked. After she had cooked this mixture down, Sook had a pot full of a slimy, gray, jellylike mixture. It stank to high heaven.

"By all that's holy, Sook," Bud would say to her, holding his nose. "If a body fell into that mess, they would come out looking like a shucked chestnut!"

Jenny would come back into the yard. "Damn you, Sook, you're stinking up the entire house with your soap," she would say. "You want soap? I got boxes of soap in the store. You take your pick. Whatever scent you want. I didn't take you off that plantation and build up my business to have you go off and boil soap like we were poor white trash sharecroppers."

But Sook never let such criticism bother her. She quietly went about her business, making soap the old-fashioned way, pouring the solution into molds, letting it harden, and then cutting the bars into hand-size cakes. None of us in Jenny's house ever dreamed of using the foul-smelling stuff. She gave it away to anyone who needed or wanted it.

As a child, I never understood why Sook took on such an unrewarding task every spring. Nothing about it made sense to me in those years. It was just one more of her peculiar eccentricities that we had learned to live with. Much later as an adult I decided that perhaps by some strange and convoluted twist of psychology, the ritual of the soap making was Sook's way of retreating into the past to the time when her father was still alive. She had been his favorite then. In those years she loved and was loved. She had had a purpose and a place in life.

Sook's major project every year, however, was the preparation of her dropsy medicine each June. When her mother, Samantha, lay on her deathbed years before, she whispered to her daughter a strange message. Sook was to visit an Indian medicine man and shaman near Clairborne who would give her a secret recipe for an Indian medicine made from herbs and roots that was certain to cure dropsy. (Dropsy is a strange disease that causes water to accumulate in the tissues, so that the person becomes bloated all over.) Samantha evidently thought that if Sook were able to make and sell this medicine, she would have some small measure of financial security.

Sook kept large sacks of strange herbs and roots in our smokehouse. Every May she and Truman scoured the surrounding woods, gathering what she needed for her medicine. What she couldn't find she purchased or bartered from her shaman friend at the Creek reservation outside Clairborne. Sook took great delight in telling us the names of the roots and herbs in her bags, but never how she used them. Some of them, such as cinchona, jalap, pennyroyal, and agave, were quite exotic, often coming from foreign countries. Sook was terribly proud of her collection.

June was Sook's month to make her dropsy medicine. Our garden would be in full bloom then. Freshly cut roses would be in most of the rooms, and their scent would permeate the entire house. Then one day we would hear from the back the sounds of a fire being made and water being poured into a large black cast-iron pot—the sounds that every June announced the start of Sook's medicine preparation.

"Jenny," Callie would demand, "why do you let that damn fool sister of ours make that vile-smelling concoction?"

"Be patient, Callie," Jenny would say. "In another week Sook will be done with her medicine. It is the only way she has of making some pocket money for herself. Go out and bay at the moon if you like, Callie. Just leave Sook alone."

Jenny then hurried out to the back steps to join the rest of the family who had gathered to watch Sook start her preparations. This was the one time of the year when Sook was "the one." She alone knew anything about the healing qualities of the herbs and roots.

Before Sook blended her various ingredients together, she would inspect them carefully. She would line up her croker sacks full of herbs and roots, then smell and pinch each item before she accepted it. Her discards went into the fire.

Little Bit would shake her head and ask, "Miz Nanny, why yo burn dem roots? Ain't dat a gawd-awful sin to waste dem?"

"No," Sook would patiently explain. "If a root is not firm and crisp, it has lost its power. My medicine must be powerful if it is to sap all that water out of a person's body. My medicine must be black as night and strong as the devil to work."

When the fire was roaring and the water boiling, Sook would start adding the herbs, roots, and other ingredients. She had about ten croker sacks lined up nearby. She would dart from sack to sack, pulling out what she needed and adding it to the big iron pot. The only one she allowed to help her was Truman. Sook boiled the mixture furiously the first day and then let it simmer the second day. She constantly skimmed a disgusting black scum off the top. Sook strained and recooked the entire mixture several times. By the end of the fourth day the mixture was coal black and putrid. The odor of that foul-smelling brew would permeate the neighborhood. Everyone on the street always knew when it was Miss Nanny's medicine-making time.

After the brew had cooled, Sook poured the black, cloudy liquid into pint-sized Mason jars and sold them for $2 each. She had a loyal clientele, including a lot of ignorant blacks and poor white sharecroppers, who traveled to our house from the distant corners of the county to buy. Sook always did a thriving business with her dropsy medicine. At one point Jenny even tried unsuccessfully to get a patent for it. Finally, a couple of local doctors started a petition and forced Sook to stop practicing medicine. She made her last batch of dropsy medicine in 1932 when she was sixty-one years old. By then I think she was ready to give up her "hankering" for making medicine. (Truman included an account of Sook's medicine making in *The Grass Harp*.)

We had in our backyard an ancient fig tree that each year yielded a bountiful supply of fruit. Sook loved figs and ate them by the dozen when they were in season. The summer when Truman was six and I was nineteen she filled her apron full of quarter-size purplish figs and carried them over to where we sat in the shade of an oak tree. She peeled the skin back from the top of a fig and then popped it, oozing and gummy, into Truman's open mouth.

"'Pon my word, Miz Nanny," Corrie called from the side window, "let dat chile do somethin' fer hisself. Yore actin' like an ole mother hen a-feedin' her own. De onliest thing is, dat chile ain't yore own a-tall."

Sook ignored Corrie and continued to feed Truman figs.

"Oh, Sook," he cried in happiness, "they are so-o-o-o good."

"I didn't get as many as I hoped to this morning because we waited until too late in the day," she told him. "The birds have eaten holes in the sides of lots of the figs."

"What about that green snake that lives near that fig tree? Doesn't he eat our figs, too?" Truman wanted to know.

Truman referred to the bright emerald-green snake that had taken up residence in our garden near the fig tree years before. We saw him often in the fig tree, wound around a limb. Sook always insisted that he was up there to eat his fill of the figs but not to worry as there were enough for all of us. Sook would never let us catch that snake or harm him in any way.

"I don't like that snake eating any of our figs," Truman pouted. "I'm going to catch that creepy thing and stomp him to death. Just you watch, Sook."

Sook suddenly became extremely agitated. "Now, Truman," she said in great seriousness and with tears in her eyes, "don't you ever harm that snake of ours. He has a right to exist, just like the two of us. The good Lord put him here in this garden for us to enjoy, just the same way He put that fig tree here. So, if you want to keep Sook's love, you show some love for that little snake."

Truman let that snake be, but he was not above having a practical joke at Sook's expense. One summer evening it was unusually quiet in the big house. The day's heat, continuing into the night, had put everyone into a lethargic mood. Jenny was toiling with her books, frowning over the figures because the red ones were too large and the black ones too small. Truman, with Sook's help, was pasting pictures into his scrapbook. Callie was flipping through the pages of a fashion magazine.

Suddenly we heard Bud call out from the back room. "Oh, my God, I just don't believe this. You all come here this minute."

Within seconds everyone was in Truman's bedroom. Bud was doubled up, laughing hysterically.

"This just kills me, just kills me," he said.

On the table in the center of the room was a head, molded from putty clay. It was quite lifelike with a forehead, nose, ears, and chin. Two marbles had been stuck in for eyes. But what was most prominent was Sook's pair of false teeth. Truman had fitted them into the lower half of the face. The shining, pearllike teeth in their pink gums set against the lifeless gray clay made an awesome sight.

Everyone, except Bud, stood there in silence. Jenny, unable to hold back a smile, looked straight ahead at the sculpture. Sook simply stroked her hands nervously. Callie gazed in open-mouth amazement. Truman glanced from one to the other, waiting to see what would happen.

"Oh, my! Oh, my!" Sook said plaintively.

"Serves you right, Sook," Jenny finally said. "I paid a hundred dollars for those damn teeth and the only thing they have ever chomped on is a glass of water."

"I think it's disgusting," Callie said, "positively revolting."

"I swear, it looks just like Jesse Mitchem," Bud insisted between chuckles. "Swear if it don't."

"It does at that," Jenny said. "You know, it's pretty good."

Truman by then was relieved. "I didn't get to finish the back, or it would have been better," he told us. "I ran out of clay."

"Oh, darling, my teeth," Sook complained softly.

"Your teeth, nothing, Sook," Jenny put in. "The only time I see them is snapping at me from a glass. May as well make *some* use of them."

Bud was still laughing. "I think I'll take this head into town tomorrow to show Jesse and the boys. They'll get a big kick out of it."

"Bud, you'll do no such thing," Jenny insisted firmly.

Truman went over to Sook and put his arms around her waist.

"I didn't mean anything, Sook, honest, and I didn't hurt your teeth. Tomorrow I'll clean them up real good and put them back in your glass just like before. I promise."

"Of course you will, darling boy, of course you will," Sook replied, kissing Truman on his forehead. But you could tell she had her doubts about how those teeth would taste and look after having been wedged into clay.

She felt most comfortable around young children, for their interests often meshed with her own. (In adult society Sook was often lost and out of place. When Jenny had a party, for example, she usually retreated to her bedroom until it was over.)

One thing Sook loved to do was to make dolls from Johnson grass. She was really quite clever about twisting and tying off the grass to make human figures and then dressing them in cute little costumes, so that each one took on a different personality.

Sook usually got Truman to go to town for her to buy the materials she needed for her doll dresses. She was much too shy to venture there by herself. I recall one spring morning when she gave Truman twenty-five cents and asked him to walk to Mr. Fripp's store and buy her some dye and pieces of muslin and gingham so that they could make dresses for the grass dolls.

Truman, who was about seven at the time, was upset. "Doll dresses!" he exclaimed loudly.

"Of course, Tru darling, doll dresses," Sook said reassuringly. "And when you get back, you can help me sew the little dresses and make the dolls. Won't we have such fun?"

"But, Sook," Truman pleaded, "dolls are for girls!"

"Don't be silly, darling," Sook persisted. "Why, just finding the Johnson grass and pulling it up is hard work. No girl would want to do that. We have to hunt the Johnson grass down and then pull it up. We have to shake the dirt off those roots and dry them in the sun, and then wash and dry them again. The roots make wonderful hair, Truman. We will have such lifelike dolls, you will not believe it."

"Aw, Sook," Truman said.

"Just you be careful, Truman, not to get Johnson grass and jimsonweed mixed up."

"Why, Sook?" Truman asked. "Aren't weeds and grass the same?"

"Shucks, Tru, they most certainly are not. Why, a body can get killed by not knowing the difference between Johnson grass and jimsonweed. Listen, now, and listen good, and Sook will explain the difference. Johnson grass smells sweet and clean. Jimsonweed stinks like the folded money a nigger keeps in his shoe all week to spend on Saturday night. And poisonous—shucks, jimsonweed can kill a horse or cow quicker than you can whistle 'Dixie.'"

Sook had Truman convinced. He took the quarter and started off toward the town square.

"Hurry on, darling," she called after him. "And when you come back, I'll have a tall glass of lemonade with a red cherry and a sprig of our mint waiting for you."

"Oh, that sounds good, Sook. But I think I'll ride my bike. It's too hot to walk."

Sook suddenly became agitated.

"No, Truman, I positively will not let you ride that bicycle on the streets. It is much too dangerous. Your little feet can hardly reach the pedals. Why, if your daddy cared a fig for you, he would never have given you such a big bicycle at your age."

"Aw, Sook," Truman complained again. "You never let me ride my bicycle anywhere except around our house and yard. That's not fair!"

"Why, darling boy, I couldn't let you out of my sight on that dangerous thing. Pshaw, you're nothing but a wee child still. What if you fell off your bicycle and bruised your head or cut your knees to ribbons, who would be there to pick you up and comfort you?"

Just then Little Bit leaned out the window. "Oh, Miz Nanny, yo let dat chile ride dat 'cycle," she hollered. "I do declare my soul, youse gwine make a sissy out o' dat boy if yo ain't careful."

"You hear me, Little Bit," Sook called back, clearly upset. "Truman will not ride any bicycle out of the yard. Not on your life, he won't." About the only time Sook could act decisively was around Negro servants and children.

"Pore chile," wailed Little Bit. "Youse gonna make a man-chile into a split-tail chile if yo ain't careful."

"Lord have mercy," Sook shrieked. "Don't you be giving yourself airs, Little Bit. Don't you forget that Jenny found you and your mother hoeing corn in a corn patch. Shucks, if it wasn't for me caring for this child, his mama and daddy might have put him in an orphans home years ago."

Then Sook dropped to her knees and gathered Truman's small frame to her bony bosom. "Tru, darling, never forget how precious you are to me," she whispered to the boy. "Nobody loves you as much as Sook does, just you remember that."

Sook was always much too protective of Truman in those years when he lived with us in Monroeville. Her imagination worked overtime, thinking up horrors that might befall Truman were she to let her guard down. For example, a popular festivity at our house was a fish fry for family and friends on the banks of the Little River. Jenny always brought along Sem, a Negro who had once worked as a chef in a dining car on the Louisville and Nashville Railway, to fry the fresh catfish Bud and the others caught. Sem built a large fire, put a big iron kettle on the coals, and fried the fish in the spitting grease in the bottom. We baked fresh corn bread and sweet potatoes and always had a blue-splattered enameled coffeepot filled to capacity.

For all of us those summer catfish fries and swimming parties were among the most enjoyable occasions of the entire year. The water in Little River was as clear as crystal. The white pebbles on the bottom were cool and smooth to the touch of our feet.

As sure as a turkey has a tail, we knew what would be said as soon as Sook told Truman about the water moccasins that she knew lurked in the water.

"Now, Tru, darling," Sook would start out, "remember to keep a close watch for those snakes. I don't want you going into deep water. You stay near shore where I can see your feet and watch out for any snakes."

"Sook," Bud would say, "you know good and well that a water moccasin can't bite when it is swimming. There ain't nothing to worry about here. You just let that boy go and have some fun."

"Shucks, Bud, don't you remember about that nigger that was swimming in Hatter's Pond and a water moccasin bit him?" Sook insisted. "Why, it took two people to pull that snake out of that nigger's thigh. And he almost died, too."

"Sook," Bud retorted, "you believe anything you hear. That nigger was not swimming when he got bit; he was walking in the marsh. And I never heard about no snake locking itself into a person's leg. It jest don't happen."

"Pshaw, I don't care what you say," Sook said. "Truman is not going to wade anywhere I can't see his feet and know he's safe from snakes."

Sook's love for Truman was almost unnatural in its intensity. In her loneliness she desperately clung to the small boy the way a drowning man clutches his piece of flotsam. Perhaps she sensed in Truman a kindred spirit. They were both forgotten people, Sook by her sisters and brother, Truman by his parents. And both were outsiders—Sook because her childlike innocence kept her apart from the adult world; and Truman because his pretty looks, delicate build, and girlish tenderness offended other people's notions of how a "real boy" ought to look and act.

Truman clung to Sook and Sook to Truman. She much preferred that he play with her than with the other children. Sook thought up endless ways to entertain Truman and fill his days. She pampered him beyond all reason, absorbing him into her own unnatural fantasy world. Much about their relationship was unhealthy.

"Miz Nanny, ain't right for yo to take up all dat chile's time," Corrie would say. "Yo let him play with de other chillun. Don't you go keepin' him so close to home all de time."

But Sook refused to listen. If the weather turned bad or the complaints of the household became too bothersome, she and

Truman would retreat to the attic. This was a favorite adventure for both of them. There they could be together in their own private world and escape completely the real world below. Our attic was a place of mystery, filled with dust and cobwebs and crammed to overflowing with old trunks, boxes of oddments, a gilt rocking horse, a tattered dress dummy, a wheelchair, and broken wicker furniture—old worthless things that counted for nothing, except to Sook and Truman, for whom they opened up new imaginary worlds. Together they searched through the boxes and barrels to bring forth from hidden places the finery of an earlier life—folded paisley shawls, fancy hand-crocheted doilies, fine linen petticoats with handmade lace and tiny, tiny tucks, even old valentines that had grown brittle and yellow with age. Sook loved to sort through the collection of old clothes and dress Truman up, putting a bonnet on his head, slipping faded white arm-length gloves on his hands, wrapping a feathered boa around his neck, and fitting his feet into embroidered slippers that had grown stiff with age. "Pshaw, Tru," she would say, "don't you look like an elegant lady ready for the ball!"

Sook and Truman would dress themselves in old clothes and play out their fantasies for hours on end. Then Sook would carefully put doilies on the arms and back of an old sofa in one corner of the attic, and the two of them would sit back and talk in the twilight for hours on end. Sook loved to tell about the past, those days when her father was alive and well. But Sook dwelled on the least attractive side of the South's history. She was full of hatred for blacks and Yankees, carrying within her all the resentment her father felt after the defeat. Her stories about that time were full of pain, cruelty, and violence; she loved the macabre, perverse, and sadistic. Fact gave way to fantasy in Sook's mind.

Sook told Truman in great detail about her father, who in her eyes became a heroic figure undone by treacherous Yankees and ungrateful blacks. She narrated how he had hauled muck from the bottom of the Alabama River to his plantation to enrich his fields. His slaves did this dangerous and unhealthy work. (Whites feared the swamps as breeding grounds for the deadly yellow fever.)

But most of the time Sook talked about blacks. Somewhere in her mind Negroes and the bad times of her father were connected. In some obscure way she blamed his former slaves for most of William's later problems, and this blame developed into a hatred for all Negroes. Sook never shared any of our respect and love for Corrie and Little Bit. To her they were servants and nothing more. Sook fascinated and often terrified Truman with horror stories of beatings, lynchings, castrations, and rapes. Her mind always went back to those things when she thought about her father and the past.

"I once heard my father tell about a nigger they caught stealing a smoked ham from their smokehouse," Sook told Truman one day. "My father called him Woot. He said he was a field hand and naturally had no rights to the yard and house the way the house niggers had. Father said he was a mean nigger with powerful arms and tiny snakelike eyes. He had been a heap of trouble on the plantation, and Father decided to teach him a lesson. Do you know what they did to him, Tru?"

"Oh, no, Sook. Please tell me. Don't keep me in suspense."

"Well, Father got a big wooden rain barrel and drove long nails through the sides. Then he forced this nigger Woot to crawl inside. Then he nailed the lid down. Then they loaded that barrel with the nigger inside onto the back of a wagon and drove to the top of a hill. Then they rolled the barrel off the back of the wagon and down that hill. Father shouted out, 'That'll teach you a thing or two, you thieving black bastard.' Three days later that nigger died from blood poisoning. But don't you go feeling sorry for that nigger, Tru, because they were all dishonest, lying, deceitful scoundrels who stole my daddy blind and cheated us out of our plantation. They were as bad for the South as those damn Yankees."

If Corrie overheard Sook telling Truman her stories, she would almost always try to stop her. "Miz Nanny, oh, Miz Nanny, don' yo go tellin' dat boy no mo' dem lies 'bout us blacks," she would plead.

"Shut your mouth, you black devil," Sook would call back. "I saw that voodoo doll you had sitting on your dresser the other day. You stay out of my business, you hear, nigger."

"May de good Jesus forgive yo, Miz Nanny, fer sayin' sich things," Corrie would cry, almost in tears.

"Sook, please don't talk to Corrie that way," Truman would ask. "She is good."

But Sook was beyond being reasoned with when it came to race. Not even Jenny's warnings had any effect upon her. "Don't you go poisoning that boy with any more of your imaginings about the other time," Jenny would holler at Sook whenever she caught her telling Truman her stories. All such warnings did was drive Sook off to the attic or some remote corner of the yard when she wanted to tell Truman about the earlier days.

Most of it was nonsense, of course. With a prime field hand costing upward of $1,500 in the 1850s, you were not about to find many owners who would be quick to toss that kind of money out the window—or into a nail-studded barrel, as the case may be. They might have rid themselves of a troublesome slave by sending him to the auction block in Mobile or New Orleans, but they were not likely to punish him in such a way as to risk his death or even serious injury. Simple economics never made much of an impression on Sook's prejudices, however. She hated blacks and loved stories in which they were tortured and killed.

Sook was, thus, a bundle of contradictory impulses. One minute she would gleefully tell Truman stories about blacks being mutilated, and the next she would bring home a baby bobcat in her apron and nurse it back to health until, spitting and scared, it would end up on top of Jenny's secretary in our living room to await the arrival of the volunteer fire department to get it down.

There was much about Sook to love and admire. Her faults were those of her place and time. She was uniquely Southern. It is hard to imagine another region of the country producing her. Sook was our burden from the past.

CHAPTER FIVE

Bud

WE ALL LOVED BUD, Jenny's only brother, this old man with his mountain of snow-white hair, his tobacco-stained teeth, and eyes almost without color. His nose was magnificently prominent, hooked to a perfect degree. We never thought of Bud as old, even though his skin sometimes had a yellowish gray tint and his kisses were always cold.

Bud's room was our refuge while we were growing up. I lost count of all the times we kids sneaked through Bud's side entrance to his bedroom to find sanctuary from Jenny's wrath. Maybe it was the first of the month and the bill from the drugstore had come in. Or perhaps it was a poor set of grades on our report cards. Or maybe we had gone on a hayride and come home at five o'clock in the morning. It didn't matter. Jenny could never enter Bud's room. That was an unspoken, but understood, rule of our household.

Jenny would come storming to Bud's door, rap on it with the full force of her umbrella handle, and holler, "Bud! Send [whoever happened to be in protective custody at the time] out! I mean it, Bud. I want them out right now, this minute! Do you hear me?"

Bud would crack the door just a bit and peer out at Jenny with a mischievous grin on his face. Then he would say in his slow voice, "My backside to you, Miss Jenny," and hurriedly close the door. And that would be the end of that.

Bud's sisters all admitted to frustration in dealing with Truman. Jenny was convinced that Truman was a hard, insensitive child whose faults were quite incurable. Callie said he was heartless and calculating. Sook insisted Truman was mystically inclined and spiritual. Bud said, laughingly, that he was possessed of the very devil.

Bud had a greater capacity for love than any of his sisters. He expressed it in odd ways, however, through wit and sly remarks. Bud was not one to broach his emotions directly. His influence on the boy may not have been as tangible as Sook's, but it was real and lasting. Bud's head was full of sage folk wisdom. I remember one day when Truman begged Jenny to let him stay home from school rather than face a teacher he dreaded. "Life is a hell of a hill to climb," Bud interjected, "but if it is too steep, get down on your hands and knees and climb it." Truman went to school that day.

The only time I recall that Bud ever scolded Truman was when he caught him stealing eggs from a wild bird's nest. He was very upset and tried to impress upon Truman the seriousness of what he had done. "Today's action proves that you have lost all the innocence of childhood because you have robbed a bird's nest of all its eggs," he told Truman sternly.

Bud always believed that there was something special about Truman. I remember when Truman left us to go to New York City to join his mother. Bud put his big, liver-spotted hand gently on Truman's head and murmured, "This boy has been blessed by God's grace. I have always felt, Truman, that someday you will be famous. I know that I will never live to see it, but others in the family will."

Bud's sole responsibility in the house was to act as host and master in the dining room at meals. He sat at the head of the table, served the plates, and kept a sharp eye on our behavior. Bud kept his walking cane—a gift from one of his Negro farm workers—close by his chair. All of us children knew that if we snickered, raised our heads, or squirmed while Bud said grace, we would get a sharp thump on the head from that cane.

Bud never attempted to set himself up independently in a profession, nor did he ever marry. There had been a parade of women through Jenny's house, but Bud never had much feeling for any of them except one of Callie's friends, a short, slim, yellow-haired schoolteacher by the name of Mattie Bell Salter. The only thing wrong with Mattie Bell's looks, as Jenny liked to point out, was that she was spider-legged. Her knees were bony and the size of small melons, and her legs below and above were like pipe stems. Mattie Bell got into the habit of taking Sunday dinner with us every week and always managed to sit at Bud's right hand. Things went smoothly until she started looking around to see how she could fit into our household. As soon as Mattie Bell began making suggestions about how the linen closets should be kept and the ways Little Bit could economize in the kitchen, Bud lost interest.

Bud always took great pride in his sisters, in seeing them well dressed, well fed, and happy. On his rare trips to Mobile or Montgomery to attend a cattle or hog auction, he would spend hours at the stores selecting gifts for them. Bud would deliberate at length over Chinese ivory fans, lace collars, pure linen handkerchiefs, and other small luxuries, but his sisters rarely appreciated such thoughtful gestures. They never realized how much pleasure Bud got from selecting gifts for them. One time he brought Callie a pair of long white French kid gloves. Instead of showing gratitude, Callie said, "Bud, don't you know long white gloves are strictly for evening wear? I never go out evenings. So what am I going to do with them?"

Bud looked perplexed. "Callie, I don't know. I'm sorry. I just thought that since you didn't have a pair, you might like some."

And after Jenny opened her box of silk stockings, she shook her head incredulously and said to Bud, "You old fool, you know damn well I handle silk stockings in the store. Why in the name of sweet Jesus did you spend good money for such things? I swear, Bud, sometimes I think you need to get your head examined."

Sook alone appreciated Bud's gifts. Once he gave her a beautiful doll with a porcelain face, blue eyes, a long batiste dress, and a poke bonnet on her jet-black hair. Sook was at a loss for words. She gathered her precious doll into her arms and disappeared into her room.

Bud knew that the doll was the perfect gift for Sook. He remembered the hard times on the Faulk Plantation when they were children. Sook's only dolls as a child had been rag dolls made from corncobs whose faces were painted with pokeberry juice. Once she had a wooden doll with jointed arms and legs that made her go out of her mind with pleasure. Never before had Sook had a doll with real hair that she could comb and brush. Unlike his other sisters, Bud was never embarrassed by the childlike antics of Sook.

I remember two things best about Bud. One was his dry, unhurried way with a story. He puckered up his facial expressions to put you in the proper frame of mind and give you a taste of what was coming. He was a marvelous raconteur and kept Truman entertained for hours. (Truman loved to sit on his lap on the porch swing and have Bud mimic everyone else in the house.) And there was, too, Bud's love and compassion for blacks. He never looked on them as just one cut above animals. He regarded them as men. He always told us that flogging a Negro was a natural outlet for passion or anger in those whites who were too cowardly to confront their own shortcomings.

Bud's pride was his "field," the 600 acres he had inherited from his father and let to Sylvester Prayer, an old black man, to sharecrop. Only when Bud escaped for a few hours from that conspiracy Jenny called "family life" and went to his cotton fields did he feel truly free. For almost thirty years he had en-joyed this innocent sanctuary.

Bud loved the land. He was a true Southern agrarian. He loved to walk up and down the rows of cotton and survey his fields, squat on the ground Indian fashion, stuff his mouth with a big plug of Brown Mule tobacco, and listen intently while Sylvester reminded him of how much fertilizer and food they had charged at Dr. Fripp's general store. (The cotton crop never paid for more than half the bill that he and Sylvester ran up there, but Bud always knew that after the bill went unpaid for so long, Dr. Fripp would tell Jenny. After her wrath had passed, she would end up paying the balance due.) Bud loved to gather a bit of his dirt in his hands and crush it between his fingers to feel its texture and watch the black stain darken his skin. If Bud loved anything, he loved his land. "Ain't nothing like land to stand by a man," he would say. "When your stomach is empty, it fills it. And when your stomach is full, well, hell, then the land is good to piss on."

Going out to Bud's field was one of the great treats of Tru-man's childhood—and mine, too. Whenever Bud went out, if he couldn't escape Truman, the two of them went together. Sometimes Truman rode on his shoulders, high in the world with Bud's whisker stubble tickling his legs. Sometimes he trot-ted beside him like a puppy, hanging onto Bud's faded blue work shirt or with one of his tiny hands clasped securely in Bud's big one.

Bud's one lifelong friend was Sylvester, who lived in an unpainted three-room log cabin at the edge of the cotton field. The windows were shuttered. The roof was made of hand-cut cypress shingles that were beginning to curl with age. A chim-ney on one side poured out a stream of thick gray smoke. A chopping block with an ax stuck in it dominated the backyard. Pigs grunted at the trough in the pigpen.

Bud and Sylvester had grown old and mellow together. Tall and black with rounded shoulders and a head that drooped forward, Sylvester seemed to look out and up toward his God. His long, thick arms hung in front in the easy, relaxed way of a wrestler. He wore his kinky hair cut short, leaving him a goodly stretch of shining forehead. Sylvester would say in his slow, backwoods drawl, "I'se heard de Lawd Gawd speak to me out dere in dis cotton patch." As he moved up and down the rows of arsenic-green cotton plants, under the throbbing blue of the summer sky, Sylvester would chant, "Weary, weary, Lawd, dis chile am weary wid life," as the blade of his hoe flashed in the sun like a heliograph.

Sylvester always gave his church two hogs every year. "I'se figure dat iffen four hundred pounds of prime pork don't keep me from burnin' in hell, den nothin' will," he would tell Bud each year when the time for his gift rolled around.

The two of them had been born in 1869, barely two months apart—Bud on March 16, Sylvester on May 2. Sylvester's father, Joshua Prayer, was still alive at the time. He claimed to be around 103 years old. He had been a slave, of course.

When Bud found Josh and Sylvester, around 1886 or 1887, they were living alone on the banks of the Little River in a shack, eating off the natural bounty of the land. Bud asked Josh why he and his son lived as they did, hidden away from everything. Josh told him that he did not believe that the slaves had really been freed. He had lost his white family in the Civil War and had hoped all those years that they would miraculously return. Josh was frightened and bewildered at not having a white family to take care of him.

Bud gave them a shack on the Faulk land. Sylvester was illiterate, never having seen the inside of a school. Bud managed to teach Sylvester to read after a fashion. The two became inseparable companions for the rest of their lives. Sylvester once told Bud that he wanted to be exactly like him. Bud replied,

"No, Sylvester, that won't do. I am a white man, and you are a black man. You're a black rascal, and that's the way I want my friend. Never try to be something you are not."

Bud, through Jenny's generosity, had always provided for Josh and Sylvester throughout those years. As a child, Truman loved to accompany Bud on his trips to his cotton field and listen while the two old men reminisced about earlier times, recalling names and deeds of friends long since dead, shrewd sayings from lips now turned to dust. As the conversation petered out, Sylvester would invite Bud and Truman back to his cabin to share whatever his wife, Charity, had fixed for lunch.

"Mr. Bud," Sylvester would say, "y'all eat some of dat hoppin' john [peas and rice cooked together] 'cause it is so much better fresh out of de pot whiles it is still breathin' off steam."

Charity was a small, chunky woman with a large face that radiated kindness. Every morning she took a broom into her front yard and swept it clean. The only thing to mar its neatness would be the tracks their chickens made as they scurried across the dusty ground.

"Chile," Charity would say to Truman, "I'se knows what yo likes. Charity ain't fergits. Y'all wants some hot biscuits wid bacon drippins an' fresh mayhaw jelly."

Neither Bud nor Truman could ever turn down Charity's invitation. Biscuits and drippings had always been a favorite treat of each. Bud would kid Truman about his mouthful of biscuit with the drippings running slowly out of the corners of his mouth.

I remember one grand Saturday morning in June of 1930 when I drove Bud and Truman out to the farm. Jenny had just bought a green four-door Chevrolet for the family's use. During the day Jenny and Callie worked in the store, Sook rarely went out and then only by foot, and Bud had never learned how to drive, preferring horses to cars. So during the day I usually had the use of the car.

The air was warm even for late June. From inside the house I heard a steady honking of the Chevrolet's horn, a warning to me that Bud was already in the front seat and impatient to be off. Saturday was always his day with Sylvester, and he would not tolerate a moment's delay.

"Wait! Wait! Don't leave me," cried Truman, as I turned the key and started the motor.

Bud and I waited until the small towheaded five-year-old climbed into the backseat and settled down.

I spun out of the driveway in my usual careless way, leaving behind a cloud of dust.

"Slow down, Tiny, damn it," Bud hollered. "You're doing ninety to the minute. Do you want to kill us?"

"I wish I could drive this old car," came a small voice from the backseat.

After twenty minutes we pulled into Sylvester's narrow dirt road and stopped in front of his cabin. The wisteria was blooming and twining around an old chinaberry tree in the front yard. At the side of the cabin a big snowball bush was in full bloom.

It was about ten o'clock in the morning. Sylvester sat on his front porch, tilting a bottomless chair back on its two rear legs, his buttocks hanging down, his feet resting on the railing. On another part of the porch sat Joshua, enjoying the morning sun. Looking older than God, Josh was completely bald, except for a fringe of hair at the back of his neck. He had pendulous jowls and a loose-lipped mouth full of crooked teeth that had gone yellow with age. His legs were long and angular. His skin was parched like the mud along the banks of the Alabama River when the water level drops in a summer drought.

Truman cautiously approached the old man, perhaps fearful that someone so very old might be brittle and thus liable to shatter upon too strong a touch. He was fascinated by Joshua's age. (I have always thought that Truman later put him into *Other Voices, Other Rooms* as the century-old Jesus Fever: "His face was like a black withered apple, and almost destroyed; his polished forehead shone as though a purple light gleamed under his skin. . . . There was a touch of the wizard in his yellow-spotted eyes—it was a tricky quality that suggested, well, magic and things read in books.")

"Hi, Mr. Joshua, how are you?" Truman shouted into his ear. "Can you hear me? Do you want to talk?"

Charity gently pushed Truman away. "Hush, chile, he can't hear yo or see yo. Ol' Joshua, he don't know nothin'. His brains is possessed wid oddments."

But Josh seemed to sense that a child was near. He opened his eyes, faded like Malaga grapes, reached into his pocket with his long, slim fingers, and slowly pulled out a jew's harp. He cupped his fingers around it and began to play. Truman started clapping his hands and swaying to the rhythm of the song. Josh's head jerked in time to the music, and one great sockless foot beat out a rhythm with a gentle slap-slap on the wooden floor of the porch. The music grew faster and faster until suddenly it died out completely. Josh had dozed off again.

In a few minutes Charity returned to the porch from her kitchen. She gently touched Josh on the shoulder and brought him back from his sleep. She began to spoon him some steaming homemade chicken broth.

When she had finished, Charity stood back contentedly. "Now, he do look spryer," she observed to us. "Dis is de onliest time his eyes lights up. It's de Lawd's hand, I allus says."

"Charity," Sylvester cut in, "youse is fergittin' yore duties. Yo ain't eber offered de friends nary a bite to eat."

Charity scurried back to her kitchen and soon reappeared with a fading Coca-Cola tray filled with mugs of steaming coffee and ropy heavy cream, heavy wedges of fresh watermelon, and a tall glass of cherry cola for Truman.

"But I like coffee," Truman protested when the glass of cola was set in front of him.

"Nah, suh," Sylvester said, "yo is no bigger'n a toad, an' drinkin' dat stuff yo is gwinter git de cawfy habit. An' iffen yo ax me, yo is gwinter be as yallow as a punkin. Chile, it will make yo sho' nuff look peaked."

We sat there on the porch, contentedly drinking the coffee and eating the watermelon, spitting the seeds into the yard for the chickens to fight over. Bud looked up and said to no one in particular, "Now, is there anything under God's roof better than this freedom and good friendship?"

Sylvester and Charity smiled, not answering in words.

Charity had spent the hours before our arrival doing spring cleaning. She reminisced about her upbringing. She could never understand how colored or white people could live with dirt. She had known people who actually had bedbugs in their mattress ticking.

"What are bedbugs?" Truman asked.

"Bedbugs is bugs dat gits in yore mattress where yo sleeps an' can be downright nasty," Charity explained to Truman. "I'se calls dem 'chinches' 'cause dey gits in de corners of de mattress an' yo can't see dem."

Charity told us that she had been raised right and had a world of things to be thankful for. Her mother never had any truck with no-account and slack-twisted black folks, or whites for that matter.

"Yas, we-uns has had a good life, me an' Sylvester. None of dat po'-folksy victuals fer us. Yo is what de good Lawd Almighty makes yo," Charity went on.

"All youse got to do is settle down in de place He has fer yo," Sylvester added.

"Sweet Jesus, ain't we all de same in de eyes of de Lawd," Charity chanted as a sort of benediction.

Bud concurred. As he grew up during those dreadful Reconstruction years on the Faulk Plantation, he had accepted all the facts of being poor. But, unlike his sister Sook, Bud did not dwell on the unpleasant and cruel memories of those years (except to flail the barbarism of slavery and the sorry impact it had on blacks). Rather he remembered the happy times the family had shared. Bud had no ambition except to live his life as he pleased, without obligations. He flew free, with malice toward none. He shared his beliefs with anyone who cared to enter his world.

Bud and Sylvester started chuckling over the time when Bud had drunk too much of their blackberry wine and decided to spend the night with them rather than attempt to get back into town. Charity had offered him a mattress she was in the process of stuffing with corn shucks she had washed and dried in the sun. Bud took the mattress and an old blanket to the corncrib. The next morning he lay there, trying to make up his mind whether he should get up. Suddenly he heard a slight rustling and felt a movement in the shucks. He said he knew instantly that he had company—a rattlesnake in his mattress. He eased himself up carefully. The snake was not coiled, and so he had time to escape. He hollered for Sylvester. The two of them gingerly grabbed the mattress and shook out a ten-pound rattlesnake with fifteen rattles. Sylvester cut its head off with an ax before the snake could escape. Bud never let Charity live that one down.

Sylvester loved to remember a time thirty-five years before when Bud had rescued him from a crowd of mean white toughs. Sylvester was a far less familiar face around town then than later, and so he was fair play for any whites with time on their hands. Sylvester had joined a group of young Negro boys and girls who had gathered behind one of the stores to swap stories. Suddenly, "Woot" Simpson, a sixteen-year-old bully, appeared with several friends, spoiling for a fight. Woot had flaming red hair and ugly, crooked teeth. He was stockily built and strong for his age. Woot carried a wet, dirty towel that he had twisted and used to snap at the legs of blacks he passed on the street, daring them to make a response.

Woot spied Sylvester.

"Now, ain't that the new nigger of Mr. Bud's?" he called out. "As I live and breathe, of course it is."

"Smack him on the legs, Woot," one of his friends hollered.

Woot snapped at Sylvester's legs with his wet towel but missed.

"Quit dat, white boy, 'cause yo ain't nothin'," Sylvester warned him.

Woot moved closer to Sylvester. His mean red eyes narrowed ominously to mere slits.

"You smart-assed nigger, you. We'll see who is nothing," Woot said between clenched lips. He snapped his towel several more times.

"Hey, boy," Woot demanded, "I want to see how you're hung. Drop those pants and give us a look."

Woot and Sylvester circled each other warily.

"Come on, boy, are you going to drop those pants of yours, or are we going to have to cut them off?"

"White boy," Sylvester warned him, "yo stay away from me or I'se gonna cut yore gizzard out." He suddenly flashed a straightedge razor he had taken from his pocket.

"Watch it, Woot," one of the other white boys said. "That nigger looks mean, like he might cut you any time."

The rest of Woot's group, about six boys, advanced menacingly toward Sylvester. Several carried broken pieces of wood they had scavenged nearby. The other blacks huddled against a wall, clearly intimidated and unwilling to come to Sylvester's defense.

Suddenly, Bud and several other white men came into view and quickly surveyed the situation. The gang of youths still advanced. Sylvester backed up against a wall, every muscle taut. The sunlight flashed off his razor blade.

"Come on, nigger, let's see what you got," Woot taunted him.

"White boy, don' vex me none. I'se tellin' yo one mo' time, don' vex me."

Again the group moved forward, but this time a lot more slowly.

Suddenly, Bud's voice stopped them in their tracks. "OK, fellows, let's see what *you've* got. Start unbuttoning. You first, Woot. Stand over there all by yourself, so we can get a good view. God damn you, boy, we want to see if you is as red down below as up above."

Bud held an ax handle in his right hand and was gently beating it against his left palm. The three white friends with him clearly intended to back him up.

"Please, Mr. Bud," Woot pleaded, "we ain't done nothing. We didn't mean any harm. Just having ourselves a joke on your nigger. That's all. Nothing more than a little joke."

"You drop those pants and drop them now or I'll use this ax handle."

There was a long moment of silence in the hot afternoon sun. And then Woot dropped his pants.

"Woot, you son of a bitch," Bud growled at him, "you leave Sylvester alone. If I hear you ever bother him again, I'll find you and crack your skull. Now pull up your pants and git."

And that was the last time Sylvester was harassed when he went to Monroeville to buy his supplies.

Every spring Sylvester and Charity rode into town on their wagon behind their mule to buy all the supplies they needed for the season's cotton crop. Bud always met them at Dr. Fripp's store, so that he could sign the bill and have it put on Jenny's account. In effect, Jenny staked Sylvester to his food, fertilizer, and seeds for the coming year. Then in September, when the cotton was harvested and sold, she would theoretically have first claim on the money. Of course, she never collected all that was due her, but then I don't think she ever expected to.

Bud and Sylvester always had excuses.

"Drat those boll weevils, Jenny. They ate up nearly the entire crop."

"Dry rot, Jenny. It got into the bales and ruined most of them. Ain't nothing Sylvester could do about it."

"That summer heat was just terrible for cotton, Jenny. Sylvester managed to save only a dozen bales."

"Damn it, Bud," Jenny would complain, "you two got more plagues than the good Lord ever visited on Job. Just one of these years you and Sylvester will do something right, and I'll get my money back. But I am not going to hold my breath on it."

Bud always felt strongly about Negroes, far more so than any of his sisters. I remember one time when the two of us had stopped off at the town's greasy spoon, a dingy little café run by a Greek who had wandered into Monroeville from God only knows where and settled down. That day while we drank our coffee, a large black man who worked for a local construction firm entered the café. He stood there for five minutes, but nobody paid him any attention. Finally he said, "Boss . . ."

"Speak up, boy," said the man behind the counter. "State your business."

"Cup o' cawfy, boss, an' a greasy, please, sir."

The white man behind the counter wiped his dirty hands on his dirty apron. "You can have the coffee and hamburger," he told the man, "but you can't eat them here, nigger."

Bud jumped up from the counter, muttering, "Damn this country," threw a dime at the man for our coffees, and stormed out of the café.

Bud even took his loving from the Negroes. From as far

back as I can remember, we all knew that Bud and Corrie had a "thing" going between them. We would hear Little Bit say to Corrie, "Y'all best git ready, 'cause Mr. Bud done got his pecker up."

We could always tell when a meeting took place. Corrie would walk up the tote road and come into the house by the side door to Bud's room. We could smell the hot, spicy gingerbread that she carried on the plate under the white linen napkin along with the aroma from the porcelain coffeepot she held in her other hand. We never knew whether they enjoyed their feast before or after their lovemaking.

In the Deep South this sort of relationship between white men and black women was common, never seen and never stopped. In our part of the South we had an expression when I was growing up: "A nigger gal can boost a white man sky high."

Corrie always said, "Mr. Bud's blood can't run hot fer no white woman. He needs de right kind o' woman to give him de right kind o' jazzin'."

Bud, too, was our family historian. He took care to pass on the accumulated anecdotes and wisdom of earlier generations of the Faulks to each new generation that came along.

I recall one Sunday in 1929. The children had to attend services at the Baptist church unless some excuse could be found that pleased Jenny. As on all other Sundays, Bud sat on the swing at the far end of the veranda. The rest of the family prepared to depart for church, but Truman was not feeling well, so Jenny said he could stay home.

Truman, sitting at the swing and picking at Bud's bony knee, suddenly asked a strange question.

"Bud, why do I live here? Why don't I live with my real Grandmother Persons or my real uncle?" he wanted to know.

Bud reached over and gently pinched Truman's ear, giving it a little wiggle. Truman knew this was Bud's gesture that meant he was loved and not to worry.

"Truman, you live here because it is your home," Bud answered.

Jenny, Callie following, walked down the steps, assuming an air of haughty reverence. "Coming, Bud?" she asked.

"Be along in a minute," Bud called back. But he had no intention of going to church. He was wound up for one of his long stories.

My excuse not to attend church having been accepted, I sat on the porch steps and listened.

"How much kin am I to you, Bud?" Truman asked.

"You're my grandson," Bud answered.

"Now I know that's not the truth," Truman said. "Tell me the truth."

"Let's see now," Bud went on. "Blood kin, you're my second cousin, thrice removed, but that's not the most important kin. The most important kin is love kin. That's why you're my grandson."

Truman knew this would bring on a story, so he said, "Tell me about it."

"Well," Bud said, as he leaned over the side of the swing and sent a long stream of tobacco juice clear over the hydrangeas, "it goes a long way back to your grandfather Arthur. He lived in Laurel, Mississippi, and his mother died very young and then his father died of tuberculosis when he was seven. Tuberculosis is . . ."

"I know what tuberculosis is," Truman interrupted. "Go ahead with the story."

Bud continued. "Samantha—that was my mother—could not go to the funeral, so I went with instructions to bring Arthur and his little brother Henderson back home. It was not easy, for there seemed to be some sort of claim on the children by the man Arthur lived with.

"He was a real devil. I found Arthur the day after the funeral in the woods tapping pine trees and collecting turpentine resin right alongside grown men.

"That Simon Legree told me, 'Hands off the boys. You lay one finger on either, and I'll blow a hole in your belly to match your mouth!' He had a big pistol at his hip to back him up. That's when I went to Cousin Lafayette Stanton, a well-known attorney in Laurel.

"He said, 'Go back home, Bud, and I promise to send the boys to you within a month.'

"Two weeks later, two little boys, shivering in the cold February weather, hopped off the mail coach in Monroeville, wrapped in overcoats that Lafayette had bought them. Arthur held out a card plaque, tied around his neck, that read: 'ARTHUR AND HENDERSON FAULK—DELIVER THESE BOYS TO SAMANTHA FAULK, MONROEVILLE, ALABAMA.'

"Samantha took the kids in right away. She said, 'You boys must be hungry. What would you like to eat?'

"'I'll eat anything,' Albert said.

"Henderson, leaning against the fireplace, said, 'Iffen I can't ha' an aig, then I don't want nuttin'.'

"From that day on Samantha kept a quart jar filled with fresh eggs packed in cornmeal. They belonged to Henderson, and everybody knew it. The boys thrived under Samantha and grew up strong and healthy.

"By the time Arthur was twelve, he was like a tiger, about as tall as a mule's hind leg with twice the kick. He could whup any man twice his size, and did it if anyone dared to raise a finger to Henderson; chew tobacco and spit with the experts; beat the champs at checkers; size up a horse in one sharp glance; and knew more about history than anyone in the county—that is, Alabama history. For history went no farther than the Alabama border. He married your grandmother when he was eighteen. And your mother, Lillie Mae, was born the next year right in our house. And this has been her home ever since. She's just like a daughter to us. That's love kin."

Truman sat quietly, pondering this.

"Bud, where did you get the Confederate sword hanging in your room?" he asked.

Bud gave another squirt of tobacco juice and settled down for another story.

"That belonged to William, my father. He enlisted on April 10, 1862, in the 36th Alabama Confederacy, Company F. He was a brave warrior and fought in many engagements. He was finally wounded at the Battle of Shiloh. Took one bullet through his back and another creased his knee."

"Was that a bad war?" Truman asked.

"Yes, Truman," Bud said slowly, "that was a bad war. And I don't want to talk about it."

Bud waited a spell and then continued.

"My father came home all broken up. People say he died spiritually on the day Lee surrendered his sword at Appomattox. His land had been pilfered, his slaves turned loose, and he had no money. This was probably the doings of scalawags, but the blame fell on Sherman. William worked hard for ten years and then just gave up. He spent the last years of his life rocking on the front porch and damning the Yankees. His war injuries hurt him all his life, and he took morphine to kill the pain. Sometimes he took too much and became dependent upon it.

"All those square miles of good farmland were left to Samantha for her small children. Jenny remembers it well, all the hard times and lean years. At seventeen she said she was tired of watching the family go nowhere except further into poverty. She decided to do something about it. No one else was capable. Her best friend was the sewing needle, but there were already dressmakers in Monroeville, so Jenny decided upon hats. She scraped together enough money, went to St. Louis, and took a course in hat designing. She must have done very well, for she was offered a job in one of the big New York stores. But Jenny's family was the most important thing to her.

"So she came back to Monroeville. She rented a small store on Main Street and started making hats for the county gentry. Her selection was full. She gave her women a garden patch of choices—grapes, cherries, carrots, radishes, roses, daisies, or a mixture. Whatever they wanted as decoration, why, Jenny would give them. They soon found it was too far to travel to Montgomery or Mobile for a good hat. Soon some of the richer hat fanciers in other cities started coming to Miss Jenny's shop in Monroeville to buy their hats. So she added stockings, skirts, coats, until her store became what you see today—complete ready-to-wear.

"You see, Tru, Jenny does it all for us. She may seem hard and cruel sometimes, but she is devoted to all of us—even more to you and your mother—you're her love kin."

Jenny and Callie came through the gate from church.

"Everybody straighten up," Jenny said. "The preacher is coming for dinner. Bud, I see you didn't make it. You missed a good sermon."

"What did he preach on?" Bud wanted to know.

"His sermon was on brotherly love," Jenny answered.

"That's strange," Bud said. "That's just what we were talking about, weren't we, Tru?"

"Yep," Truman answered.

CHAPTER SIX

Corrie
and Little Bit

ONE OF THE BEST-KNOWN and beloved Southern institutions was the black "mammy." Hollywood films often reduced this figure to caricature and stereotype, but she was, nonetheless, a real and significant force in the lives of many Southerners, profoundly influencing their development. In the South of an earlier time it was customary for many families of middle and higher incomes to employ a nurse to help raise the children. Often the "mammy" was hired at the birth of the first child and remained with the family until the last child had grown and left home.

Lillian Smith in her book *Killers of the Dream*, an autobiographical account of growing up in the Depression South, says of the black "mammy": "Her role in the family was involved and of tangled contradictions. She always knew her 'place,' but neither she nor her employers could have defined it. She was given limited authority, but it was elastic enough to stretch into dictatorship over not only the children but the white mother and sometimes even the male head of the family as well. . . . She was a necessary part of these big sprawling households; and her value extended far beyond child rearing. She nursed old and young when they were sick, counseled them when they were unhappy, took the problem child at least out of earshot, and in crises her biologically rooted humor had a magic way of sweeping white clouds away. She was a nurse, witch doctor, and priest, conjuring away our warts, our stomach-aches, and fears, all of which simply disappeared when she said they would."

In Jenny's household there was no "mammy" as such, but we had Corrie, our black house servant, and Little Bit, our black cook, both of whom had lived on the premises for as long as I could remember. They had started working for Jenny shortly after she built her store and big house at the turn of the century. By the time I moved in they were every bit as much a part of the household as Bud, Sook, and Callie. I don't know what Jenny paid them—probably no more than $5 a week, if that. But she took care of all their needs, and whatever clothes they wanted they got free from her store.

Little Bit was a huge hunk of woman with the agility and cunning of a Siamese cat. She was part Cajun, part Indian, and part Negro. Or, as she boasted, "Just a li'l bit of everything." (If she had any regrets, it was about her Indian ancestry. "I'se jist naturally hate dose Injins," she would say, especially when the subject of Lillie Mae's attachment to Teshu came up. "Iffen dose Injins had left de French an' Scotch in me, I'se could pass for white. Damn to hell dose Injins for spoilin' a good mix.")

A deep scar ran across her left cheek from the tip of her ear to her chin. As unsightly as it was, the livid scar did not detract that much from her oval-shaped cameo face, accentuated by long black hair parted in the middle and combed over her temples to conceal all of the ear except the tip of her lobe. For so slender a face her mouth was startlingly full and red-lipped. Little Bit was really quite a handsome woman. She did not know her age. "I'se figures I'se 'bout Miz Jenny's age, more or less," she would say thoughtfully. "But I'se cant's be certain. Ain't nobody eber kept no records on birthin' of blacks in dose days." (Recently, when I started to set down my recollections on those times for this book, I suddenly realized that none of us ever knew her real name.)

Little Bit's love for men was no secret. At the drop of a hat she would say, "Dere's no sweeter place to lay for love dan in a fresh haymow. Gawd, jist smellin' dat mixture of horse an' hay is purely like bitin' into unexpected pepper." When we asked her why she always made love in an enclosed barn, Little Bit would shake her head and answer, "De ground always looks shaky in de moonlight. I'se fearful of de long branches of dose trees. Dey goin' reach right down an' pull me up to Gawd knows where. More dan likely plat-eyes an' spirits run round de ground. De ground ain't no place to take yore lover at night!"

Little Bit lived in the house, in a small bedroom just off our kitchen. She had her hands full just feeding our household. She was an excellent cook. "Lord," Bud would say when Little Bit had one of his favorite dishes cooking away on her stove, "people gnaw their fingers and bite their tongues just to get a smell of the steam when she raises them pot lids!"

One of our favorite dishes was creamed cabbage. Little Bit would hand-shred the cabbage very fine, cook it until it was tender, and then season it with sour cream, vinegar, white and black pepper, and butter. When she cooked, she often sang and danced.

I recall one afternoon when I walked in on her unexpectedly. I was old enough then to work in Jenny's store most of the day. As I came through the house, I could hear Little Bit in the kitchen, tapping her feet and clapping her hands. When I stepped into the kitchen, I saw her dancing lightly over the kitchen floor in step with the song she was singing.

> "De mans I love he up an' goes.
> 'Bout all I'se got is worries an' woes.
> I git de fever, I git de chills.
> I git de misery, I git de ills
> I got de doggone, low-down lovesick bl-ue-ues."

Little Bit looked up and saw me standing in the doorway.

"Why, Miz Tiny, I'se never knowed yo was home. Yo ain't sick, is yo?"

"No, I just decided to take the rest of the day off," I told her.

I stayed in the kitchen. Little Bit fixed me a late lunch. We chatted—about her current boyfriend, Lillie Mae and Teshu, and other family matters.

And, of course, Truman. Jenny was worried because his grades in school had been so low. "I'se tells yo, Miz Tiny, ain't no use worryin' 'bout dat boy," Little Bit said. "I'se thinks he is gwine be a writer. Go an' read some of dat stuff he done writ on de sidewalks 'bout people here 'bouts. He uses dat li'l wooden box full wid de white chalk dat Miz Jenny give him las' Christmas. Lawd! Dat boy can be mean. He is a real name caller. Dat boy is shorely gwinter grow up an' writes 'bout people."

"Little Bit," I finally asked her, "you promised me once that you would tell me someday about how you got that scar on your face. What happened?"

"Chile, youse is a caution. Dat was a long time ago when I was young an' spirited. I was at a big dance wid my man, an' dis damn floozy bitched-assed nigger started dancin' an' makin' eyes at my man. De first thing I knows dey was gone. When my man comes back I axed him 'bout it. 'Stead of my man tellin' me, this floozy spoke up an' says to me, 'Don't come whinin' to yore man. He done found somethin' better.'

"I knowed dis was true. Weren't no use me tiradin' 'bout it. Dat whore was grinnin' an' beamin' like she had inherited Gawd's kingdom. I knowed what had happened.

"I'se waited. Praise His name, I'se sees dat gal was off in a corner byes herself an' den I pulls out my razor an' lit in on her, slashin' her up an' down. Dat gal was beginnin' to look like a piece of chopped meat."

Little Bit was jumping up and down and jabbing with her

cooking fork as if she were a swashbuckling Douglas Fairbanks. "Take dat, yo bitch, an' dat, an' dat," she hollered.

"OK, Little Bit, but how did you get *your* scar?" I insisted.

"Hold onto yore patience, chile, I'se jist 'bout to tell yo dat. Well, I was slashin' an' cuttin' on dat whore when dat crazy nigger give me one cut wid her razor on my face. But dat ain't nuttin'. Miz Tiny, yo shore 'nuff should have seen dat floozy. Ain't no man eber want her agin, dat is, if dey eber got her put back together agin."

Somehow I never could imagine our gentle, good-natured Little Bit wielding a razor in a dance-hall brawl. But then I remembered another story she told us about an experience she had had as a young girl. Once she had been surprised by a vagabond white man who had tried to rape her on her parents' little farm. She broke away, ran back to the yard to her father's big hay rake, and jerked out one of its eighteen-inch spikes. The man caught up to her. Little Bit waited until he was right beside her, and then she suddenly stabbed him in the back with the long spike. He screamed and fell to the ground. Little Bit ran off. When she returned, the man was nowhere to be seen. She never knew what happened to him. That was the only story about those times that Little Bit ever told us. She did not like to talk about her youth.

By the time Little Bit had finished telling me how she had gotten her scar, the afternoon was more than half gone. Suddenly, Truman burst through the kitchen's rear door, all excited. "Little Bit, give me a big bucket of water, please," he demanded.

"Chile, what's youse wants wid a bucket of water?"

"A gypsy man and woman are on the road in front in a covered wagon," Truman explained. "They told me they are very thirsty and asked me for some water for them and their horse."

"How's youse knows dey is gypsies?" Little Bit asked.

"'Cause they look like gypsies. They have dark skin. And the woman is wearing a bright-colored dress with a red and yellow bandanna around her head. Oh, Little Bit, please hurry. I know a gypsy when I see one. I have seen lots of them in my life. In fact, someday when I am grown up, I may decide to be a gypsy and ride all over the country and do just what I please. So don't waste time and get me that bucket of water, real quick, or I'll tell Jenny on you."

"Boy, don't yo come in here mouthin' off at me. Yo'll git yore bucket of water iffen yo don't let dem gypsies put dere dirty moufs on it.

"An' another thing, Mister Smarty, best be kerful," Little Bit warned Truman as he struggled to carry the bucket of water out the back door. "Yo can't trust a gypsy no more dan yo can spit to Mobile. Why, dey can spirit yo away an' we never see yo agin for eber an' eber."

Truman gave Little Bit his nastiest look as he disappeared through the door.

"Miz Tiny, yo best sneak round on de porch an' see what's goin' on," Little Bit cautioned me. "I don't trust no gypsies."

I took her advice and put myself unobtrusively on our front porch to survey the proceedings. I watched Truman hand the bucket of water to the woman. She reached back into the wagon for a gourd dipper.

She and her husband drank long and full from the bucket. "Thank you, young man," she said when she had finished. "Kindness like that will surely be rewarded. You will go to heaven on a shooting star."

Her husband took the bucket around to the front of the wagon to let their horse drink.

"How old are you, young man?" the woman asked Truman.

"Six and a half," he answered.

"My, but you are bright for such a young boy," the gypsy

woman said. "How would you like to go to Mobile with us? Have you ever seen Mobile?"

"Of course, many times," Truman replied. "I was born in New Orleans and get around quite a bit. But I don't want to go to Mobile with you."

The woman handed the bucket back to Truman.

"Are you certain?" she persisted. "It's lots of fun riding in this here wagon. We'll show you the world."

"No, thanks."

The woman thought a moment while her husband adjusted their horse's harness.

"Well, boy, do you have any money?" she asked Truman.

"Sure I have."

"Bet you don't have two bits in your pockets."

Truman reached into his pants pocket and pulled out a shiny quarter. "See," he said, and held it up.

"Tell you what," the woman said. "Would you like to see the pot of gold at the end of the rainbow?"

The gypsy man gave his wife a hard jerk on one arm.

"You idiot, what the hell are you trying to do?" he growled. "Get us arrested? You got us jailed in Perdue Hill for that damn stunt. Just lay off the kid."

"Shut up," she snapped back. "I know what I'm doing. And we can use the two bits. This is a nice kid. He won't do anything."

The woman turned back to Truman.

"Give me your two bits, young fellow, and I'll show you the pot of gold at the end of the rainbow," she promised Truman. "And if I don't, you get your money back. Fair enough?"

"Well, OK," Truman said skeptically. He handed her his coin. "Now let me see that pot of gold."

"Sure enough, young man," the woman said. "Here you go. Don't blink or you'll miss it."

The woman stood up in the end of the wagon and grabbed hold of her long skirt. She suddenly pulled up the front to well above her waist. She was stark naked from the belly down. Her pubic hair had been dyed a brilliant gold. She stood for a few moments, shaking her crotch in Truman's face. Then she dropped her skirt.

"Now," she told Truman, "don't you let anyone tell you that you haven't seen the *real* thing."

The man pulled her back into the wagon. He gave the horse a good slap with the reins. "Get up, Jupiter," he called out. "Get this fool woman out of this town before we get locked up again."

The old horse trotted off slowly, leaving Truman standing behind in a daze.

The back flap of the wagon slowly opened enough for two small heads to peep out. There was a young boy about five and a little girl about three. They both had drawn faces and dark, sad eyes. As the wagon turned the corner toward the road leading to Mobile, they both held up a tiny hand in a solemn farewell.

When Truman was young, he had some of the richest experiences of his life in Monroeville. There's no doubt of that.

Corrie Wolf, second in command after Little Bit, was a light coffee-colored black woman with a well-rounded rump and a fine pair of breasts. She always looked raunchy and ready. Corrie was a quadroon. She lived in a little house behind our big house in the old slave quarters down the "tote road," so called because the slaves once used that road to return each day to their quarters, "toting" all kinds of food from the kitchen at their master's house.

Little Bit looked on Corrie as a heathen. Corrie saw Little Bit as the "image of God in ebony." (This was hardly fair because Little Bit, although not as light-skinned as Corrie, was still

considerably lighter than most other Negroes in Monroeville.)
There were always strong undercurrents between Little Bit and
Corrie. Each ruled her own domain and was loved and respected
by the rest of the household. Corrie, however, was much more
of a character than Little Bit, always poking her nose into everybody's business.

Corrie was very much a woman, but at the same time she
had some mannish qualities. Her broad shoulders, loud voice,
shrill whistle, and curses all recalled a man rather than a woman.
Her weaving walk always reminded me of the lumbering steps of
a sailor just in from two months at sea. She loved to tell us
stories, and they often combined a masculine toughness with
the observations of a smart, cynical woman. Corrie knew that
life was a fight, and she was fit for it—vigilant, brutal, and
clever when the occasion demanded. She proudly wore the scars
of battle. The several teeth she had had knocked out in a fight
with a former lover years before were one such mark of a life
that had left her with little innocence or softness.

Corrie practiced voodoo. She claimed to be a direct de-
scendant of one Dr. Yah Yah, a voodoo doctor in New Orleans
who had enjoyed a considerable reputation back in the 1850s.
Corrie insisted that Dr. Yah Yah had been born with a caul in
his hands as a gift from God. She was always making crosses out
of red root and hanging them at our front door to block the
passage of evil spirits into our house. And she put fresh pepper-
mint inside all our pillowcases for added protection.

Children brought up in the South during the first half of
this century were weaned on tales of "hants," spirits, plat-eyes,
and ghosts. Black people lived in a universe made all the more
frightening by the presence of a host of devils, witches, and
bad-luck spirits. Corrie was no exception. She was full of black
folk wisdom passed down to her from earlier generations.

"Don't y'all spit in de fire," Corrie would warn us children.
"It will dry up yore lungs."

"Iffen yo get bitten on de ear by a snake, yo will understand de language of de birds."

"It will muddle de mind of a chile iffen dey sleep in the full light."

"Don't yo eber plant a cedar tree 'cause when it gits big enough to shade yore grave, yo is gone die."

"Don't go out of de house on a dark night 'cause de branches of a tree will reach down an' carry yo away."

Another favorite of Corrie's was "bottle trees." There were always several around her cabin and Jenny's house. Corrie regarded them as indispensable in her constant war against the evil spirits rampaging through the world, ready to threaten any innocent folk foolish enough to lower their guard. She would take a blooming tree (crape myrtles were a favorite) and insert the ends of its branches into bottles. "Dis here is positive protection agin de evil spirits," Corrie patiently explained to me one morning, as she went about the business of putting her bottles on a blooming shrub in Jenny's backyard. "Yo sees, chile, de evil spirits come to de house, ready to cause mountains of mischiefs. Only 'fore dey gits in, dey sees first de bottle trees. Dey is 'tracted to de bright colors an' comes to 'vestigates. Dey comes closer an' closer. An' den, first thing yo knows, dey is trapped inside dat bottle an' can't eber git out agin."

Corrie had quite a reputation among the local blacks for her ability to work magic and voodoo and was often in demand. She had a special string of beads used for aiding labor when a woman was about to give birth. Corrie claimed they had come all the way from Africa and had been passed down to her by way of her illustrious predecessor Dr. Yah Yah. No matter how the baby came into the world—feet first, head first, or sideways—those beads would speed it safely to its mother's bosom. They looked like unpolished amethysts, rubies, and emeralds.

Often at night Corrie would find herself aroused from a deep sleep by a frantic knocking on her front door. Always there would be a distraught man, colored or poor white, standing there. "Come on, Corrie, git yore birthin' beads quick like an' come wid me, fo' Gawd's sake. Dat gal a-gwine die iffen yo don't," he would tell Corrie.

"It's de truf," she would tell us later. "But I wishes dem beads had been give to somebody else 'ceptin' me. Iffen I lost dem beads I'd be ruint fo' true."

The first thing that Corrie did upon arriving at the shanty where the woman was in labor was to place the beads around the girl's neck, making certain they touched her naked skin, and then pull them down tightly between her breasts. Corrie then drew the quilt or blanket snugly up under the girl's neck and left, allowing no one else to enter the room.

Later, after the beads had worked their magic, Corrie would assist in the actual birth. She always had some fresh spiderweb handy, "'cause a life can leak out fast an' de spiderweb can dam it up an' hol' it fast." She would caution the mother against giving the child the wrong name, for that would most certainly cause it great mischief in life, if not an early death. And Corrie always took account of the tide and the moon. They had to be just right. A child born at new moon would be contrary and troublesome all its life. Any child born on the rising tide would more likely be a male.

Next Corrie would have a man get her a good sharp ax. The blade had to be clean without any rust. This she placed under the woman's bed to cut the labor pains. (Rust on the blade, however, would make the labor long and drawn out.)

Once the child had been born and safely delivered to the care of its mother, the celebrations began. In Rooktown the night of a birthing was always cause for a party. All the neighbors chipped in with food and drink. There was singing and dancing. Open fires roared under large black kettles.

"I'se got a whole hawg an' a bushel o' rice a-cookin'," a yellow Negro man with a pockmarked face would holler out, as he stirred his big iron kettle. "Ev'ybody git good an' hongry while dat gal inside is possumin'."

"Chitterlins an' pig's feets," a woman at another table would call out, "spare ribs wid fatback."

As soon as Corrie announced the sex of the child to the gathered crowd, the dancing would begin and last until the early hours of the morning. A makeshift band would form at the last minute—guitars, banjos, drums, and jew's harps—whatever was available.

"Git yore pardners 'cause de music is gwine tickle a preachin' man's toe," a caller would holler. "Swing yore own true love."

Every skirt was spinning and twirling.

"Sashay all!"

Corrie rarely stayed for very long at these birthing parties. She insisted they usually lasted too long and got out of hand too quickly. Too much bootleg corn whiskey was bad for tempers, and fights were common. "De trouble is dat dey ain't content to wallow wid de hawgs," Corrie would say contemptuously. "Dey is got to start cuttin' one another wid dose razors." (She had been slashed by a straightedge razor at one of these parties years before.)

Perhaps I ought to say a few words here about Rooktown. Corrie, like most of Monroeville's other better-class Negroes, looked down on the place and rarely had anything to do with the people there. Rooktown was a shantytown a couple of miles outside Monroeville proper. It sat in a low depression. During the rainy season the dirt streets would be pools of water for weeks on end. The trees about Rooktown were a popular nesting ground for ravens, which is how the settlement got its name.

Rooktown's population was about evenly divided between poor whites and poor blacks, who lived in twenty or so shacks scattered haphazardly along the road. Most of the blacks did odd jobs about town—yard work, window washing, whatever came along. Most of the white men worked off and on in a nearby sawmill. Monroeville's only prostitutes lived and worked in Rooktown, much to the distress of the church ladies.

Rooktown was a collection point for the flotsam of local society. This is where you ended up, white or black, when you were down on your luck and flat on your back. Few of the men held steady jobs or had any ambition for regular work. Most lay around during the day, sorting out their fishing rods, straightening their fishing hooks, and doctoring the sores on their mangy hunting dogs. Hand-cranked gramophones blared out randy tunes. The men got drunk together, fought one another, and whored with their neighbors' wives.

Every Sunday afternoon an itinerant preacher arrived in Rooktown to hold a church service at a different shanty. His name was Teet. No one ever knew his last name. He was the blackest African Negro I ever saw. He always passed the hat, actually a small metal wash bucket. If any members of the congregation refused to toss in a coin (and Teet could always tell by the sound when a contribution was made and how large it was), he would threaten them with hell's own fires. "Wallow on de ground an' pray," Teet would exhort his crowd. "Pray hard as yo kin 'cause de spirit is workin' on yo." After a few years Teet was run out of Monroe County when he was discovered fooling around with a white girl in Rooktown. The townspeople were rather casual about the affair, and no KKK members marched into Rooktown bearing torches and crosses. Everyone figured that no white girl would have any chance for respectability living in a pesthole like Rooktown.

Rooktown was where the white boys and men shopped whenever they wanted easy sex. The girls who lived there all had bad reputations. Sometimes you gave them a few coins. Other times you just took what they had to offer.

The white children from Rooktown who attended the town

school were usually segregated on one side of their classrooms. Few of the other students ever had anything to do with them. The Rooktown children were dirty. Their clothes smelled of urine. Their scalps crawled with lice.

Most Southern towns in the first half of the century had their Rooktowns. Their names may have differed—Crackertown, Mudtown, Niggerville, or Black Street. But they all had a sameness about them. They represented the absolute bottom, society's garbage dump.

All of us children at Jenny's house loved to visit Corrie in her house down the tote road and hear her stories of the Old South that she loved to tell. "Mind yo chillun don't step on dat phlox," she would warn us as we walked through her yard. "Hit's been here 'fore I could remember." Confederate jasmine covered the banisters along the small porch. A pink rambling rose climbed up the hand pump on the back porch. A lilac tree grew alongside her chicken coop. Corrie kept a small vegetable garden. Nearby was an old trellis covered with concord grapes. A struggling apple tree with worm-eaten fruit stood in the far corner of her yard.

Inside the cabin everything was neat and tidy. Corrie kept a fire going most of the year in her limestone fireplace. She had a long pine window box where she stored her handmade quilts and corn-shuck pillows. The rest of her furniture consisted of two cowhide chairs, a bed, and a table. A set of iron pots was stacked up near the fireplace. A big hoecake spider pan and one small shallow iron frying pan hung on the wall. Corrie draped long strings of red peppers over her ceiling beams. "Pepper makes a man warm-blooded an' kind," she used to tell us. "Don't youse gals eber fergit dat when youse starts cookin' for yore own man."

Corrie's cabin offered her some solitude and peace after the hustle of Jenny's house. "I'se needs some time to belongs to myself," she would tell us when she took off to go home. She loved to sit in her backyard and churn her own butter (Bud had given her a pied cow from his farm). Every summer she would pick the bold blue huckleberries that grew nearby. Corrie never worried about the rattlesnakes that always seemed to thrive wherever berries flourished. She never ventured forth on a berry-picking expedition without her snake charmer—a small pink pig, tied to the end of a rope, that squealed every step of the way. When she did find a rattlesnake, she always killed it and then saved the rattles to hang around a baby's neck to make its teething easier.

Corrie had the use of an ancient spring house at the far edge of Jenny's property near her own little cabin. There she kept her butter and milk. No one else used the spring house. Yellow jasmine sprawled over the top, casting tendrils every way and knitting the air into a green curtain.

Corrie loved to sit in front of her fireplace and pop popcorn. She grew her own. Every spring she planted a row of popcorn plants. She carefully shaped the small hills and punched four corn seeds into each one. She chanted as she planted her corn:

> *"Four grains to de hill—*
> *One fer de cutworms,*
> *One fer de rot,*
> *One fer de crow,*
> *And one fer to grow."*

There was one place in Corrie's backyard we were not permitted to approach. That was the climbing rosebush she called the "Seven Sisters." Corrie claimed that she could hear a constant "thump, thump, thump, thump, thump, thump, thump" (always seven) coming from the ground during the day but that the noise stopped at night.

We asked Corrie what those thumps that she heard meant.

"Why, shorely, chillun, yo knows dey is seben daid peoples

under dat rosebush," she cautioned us. "Dat's a fac'. Don't yo never dig round dat bush. Iffen yo do, dem ghosts will rise out of dat dirt an' hant me de rest of my born days."

When we ate at Corrie's house, she served us collard greens (Jenny never allowed them in her house because of their bad smell) cooked with fatback, the fatty side of a hog. There would usually be a pot of hot mash made with freshly ground corn and sweet potatoes that she had baked in the gray ashes of her fireplace.

"Eat a-plenty, chile," Corrie would tell Truman. "I'se wants yo to grow. Put some pot likker from de greens on yore mush. Sweet 'taters an' fatback meat fatten yo up fast enough. Yo is goin' on seben years old, but yo don't looks dat old. I'se hopes to Gawd dat you ain't no runt."

"I am not a runt," Truman would answer, haughtily. "And besides, I don't like sweet potatoes. I am not going to eat them."

"Chile, yo talks so much, someday yo is gonna miss an' bite yore tongue in two. Den what yo gwine do? I ax yo, what yo gwine do?"

"Corrie," Truman said, "you talk funny. Do you like being black?"

Corrie nodded and answered, "Gi' me de black all de time. White t'ings is too weakly."

"I'm not weak, thank you, Corrie," Truman answered quickly.

"Why, chile, I'se bet yo can't kill no mosquito. All a black person has to do is git some sweat out of dere armpits an' rub hit on yore face. Dat'll run dem bugs. Boy, black is strong."

Corrie glanced over her room and saw Truman's sun hat on her bed. She was horrified.

"Chile, don't yo eber put no hat on a bed. Dat will only bring yo bad luck. Iffen yo have to, den stick a sharp pin through it 'fores yo do. Den youse safe."

Truman's grandfather,
Arthur Faulk, and
grandmother, Edna Marie
Faulk, with their
children—Mary Ida
(between her father's
knees), Truman's mother,
Lillie Mae (standing
between her parents),
Marie (in front of Lillie
Mae), Seaborn (seated on
steps), and the infant,
Lucille.

Truman's mother,
Lillie Mae Persons Capote,
in the 1920s.

Truman with his real father, Archulus Persons, in Monroe, Alabama, about 1930.

Lillie Mae and Marie Rudisill at the Mardi Gras in New Orleans, about 1930.

Lillie Mae before her marriage,
about age eighteen.

Lillie Mae and Teshu, her
Indian lover, on a bank of the
Alabama River in Claiborne,
Alabama.

Truman with his distant cousin Sook Faulk, Jenny's sister. Sook was like a mother to Truman, and was his all-time favorite.

Truman as an infant.

Virginia Herd Faulk, known as Jenny, about 1895. Though only a very distant relative, Jenny was Truman's sole provider for his first seven years.

Nelle Harper Lee—Truman's closest childhood friend.

Truman's real father,
Archulus Persons, in 1975.
Persons always resented
Truman's taking of the name
Capote instead of his own.

Truman at age eighteen
while visiting his father in
Monroe, Louisiana.

Jenny Faulk, Truman's distant cousin, at eighty.

Truman's stepfather, Joe Capote, with Lillie Mae at Versailles shortly before she committed suicide.

Truman in December 1966.

"You're not sticking any old pin in *my* hat and that's that," Truman insisted.

"I jist can't stand a no-mannered boy-chile," Corrie said wearily. "I'd skin yo alive iffen yo was mine."

Truman at this point was ready to cry, but Corrie picked him up and plunked him down on her bed, stacked high with three puffy goosedown mattresses, and slipped a huge cornshuck pillow under his head. Then she brought him a small plate with his greens and a sweet potato dripping with fresh butter. Corrie fed him like a baby until Truman had finished his meal. A few minutes later he dozed off contentedly.

Corrie's ways may have seemed rough at times, but she actually had an immense amount of love for all of us. Lillie Mae was her favorite, and she watched her like a hawk. "For shore, dat Lillie Mae acts like she got her tail full o' turpentine," she would tell Little Bit. Then Corrie would think a moment. "'Course, hit's her own tail an' she kin do wid it as she pleases."

If Corrie caught any of us in a lie, she would say in disgust, "Dat tale jist don't wash."

Corrie was our magic carpet into a wonderful world of black folk heritage that was closed to most white children. The ordinary became wondrous when perceived through her rich imagination. We never knew what surprise she would spring on us next.

For example, her "fever eggs" had been used by many people, both white and black, in town, most of whom would have denied it vehemently had you asked them about it. Corrie got her "fever eggs" from a hen that was ready to lay an egg. She would grab the unsuspecting bird off her nest, tie her feet together, and hang her upside down in the dark for exactly two hours, all the time saying prayers for the sick person. Then the hen was put back on her nest, where she immediately expelled her egg. Corrie used only the white of the egg, rubbing it into the hair of the fever-ridden person and leaving it there until the fever disappeared, ideally the following day.

Not everyone approved of such pagan doings, of course. One day Bud, Truman, and Corrie were accosted on the street by Miss Effie Mae Mitchem, our resident bluenose busybody, as they returned from a trip to Mr. Fripp's general store. She was a wizened woman of sixty or so but still as lively as a sparrow going after bread crumbs near a picnic. She was the principal at the local school. Miss Mitchem was always butting her nose into other people's business.

"Bud, do you think it is wise for a small child like Truman to be around Corrie?" she demanded in the tone of voice that local moral authority always seems to assume when talking about someone whose behavior offends them.

"Now, Effie Mae . . ." Bud tried to protest.

"Really, Bud, don't you think you are being just a little too democratic?" Miss Mitchem went on. She talked the entire time as though Truman and Corrie were not there. "I mean old families should stick together, as it were, and not do anything to bring in disrepute and create scandalous incidents for the town to talk about."

"Effie Mae," Bud said in a weary voice, "what in the name of sweet Jesus are you getting at?"

"Well," Effie Mae began slowly, "that house servant of yours . . . she's a bad influence on that boy. She believes in ophiology."

"Now, what the hell is this *ophiology*?" Bud asked, beginning to get angry.

"*Ophiology*," Miss Mitchem stated in her best schoolmarm tone of voice, "is the study of snakes. Unfortunately, Corrie's interest is less than academic. That woman comes close to being a snake worshiper. And everyone about town knows that she practices voodoo."

There was a long period of shocked silence on Bud's part.

"I think you had better keep a sharp eye on that servant of yours, Bud," Miss Mitchem continued.

"Now, look here," Bud barked. "Corrie is not a witch. She is not a voodoo priestess. She does not conduct occult rites. And you had better apologize to her right this moment."

Corrie had been following the discussion closely. You could tell it took all her effort to keep her temper under control.

Miss Mitchem was like an old bulldog. She refused to give up.

"If that woman does not believe in voodoo, then why does she wear that thing she calls an amulet of saints' toes around her ankle?" she demanded, pointing to Corrie's feet.

"Effie Mae!" Bud shouted. "End this conversation right now! It's like talking about somebody's privates! You go off and mind your own business."

As Miss Mitchem stormed off, Corrie hollered after her, "Old white lady, yo watch out fer de next fiery-hot day when de sun drops down in de sky at de end likes a ball of blood. Dat's an omen. A bad omen! Yo best watch out an' stay inside yore house. 'Cause dat means bad luck is a-comin' at yo like bunches of grapes!"

I remember many a happy afternoon when we all sat around the big kitchen table listening to Corrie's tales of the carpetbaggers, Yankee soldiers, and slavery. She had been born shortly after the close of the Civil War into a family of former slaves. Her father, Tobias Wolf—he had taken his name from his owner (a common practice: there are lots of Negroes today in Monroe County with the name of Faulk)—had gone through sheer hell during the Civil War. His owner lived on a big plantation in another part of Alabama (Corrie never knew where), and local white trash was mistakenly convinced that he knew the location of vast treasures of family silver buried somewhere near the big house to keep it out of the hands of the Yankee soldiers. They tormented him repeatedly, trying to get him to reveal the location of the silver.

As Corrie sat with her coffee cup in front of her, working her way through her story, she would drop a little more molasses into the coffee to sweeten it. Corrie's own preference was for stories about the atrocities committed on young defenseless black girls in those chaotic years after the Civil War. She always started out by shaking her head and saying, "Dere ain't no latch on a black gal's door."

When Corrie began with those kinds of thoughts, Jenny would try to head her off into something more pleasant if Truman was listening.

"Corrie, tell them about something happy that happened," she would urge her. "Tell them about Toby's sugarcane-grinding parties."

But we never wanted to hear about the good times. Rather we wanted Corrie to scare us with stories about how she had suffered at the hands of carpetbaggers or to hear of the terrible things done to runaway slaves captured in the swamp.

Corrie loved to tell us about the time when a small band of deserters from the Confederate army dragged her father, Toby, into the swamp and tortured him. They wanted to know where his master had buried the family silver and jewels. Enough plantation owners had done just that, so stragglers from both armies were continually looking for caches.

According to Corrie, two men tied Toby to a tree and then stripped his shirt off his back. Another approached him, a nasty-looking bullwhip in his hand.

"Nigger," the man demanded, "where did your master bury his silver?"

"Don't know, massa, dat's de Gawd's truf," Toby pleaded.

The whip suddenly whirled out to strike against his back, raising a deep red welt.

"Where's the money, nigger?" the man asked again.

"Please, white man, I'se jist a dumb nigger. I'se don't know nothin'."

The whip struck again and again. Toby screamed after each fall of the lash. In a few minutes his back was crisscrossed with over two dozen stripes, many of them oozing blood in the yellow light of the lanterns.

"Nigger," someone called out.

The sagging head moved slightly but did not make a reply.

"Give me the whip," one ragged man said. "I'll see if he is still alive."

"I can speak, massa. Please don't hit me agin."

"Do you know where the silver and money is hid?"

"No, massa, 'fore Gawd, I'se don't."

"Do you know what happened to the livestock?"

"No, massa, 'fore blessed Jesus."

The men discussed the situation and then decided Toby had been punished enough. If he did know the location of the buried treasure, he would die before he revealed that information. They could always come back another day and try him with something else.

And return they did. That was another one of Corrie's stories. The same group grabbed Toby a second time and chained him to the roots of a mangrove tree exposed during low tide. (That information always convinced me that Toby had belonged to a plantation down along the coast, probably not far from Mobile.) They told him that he had until high tide to tell them where the treasure was buried or he would drown.

"Den I'se reckoned I'se goin' be drowned," Toby replied.

"Where's the silver?" one of the men asked him, giving him a hard kick in the stomach at the same time.

"Massa, please, I'se tolds yo 'fore. I don't know nothin' 'bout no silver."

"Nigger, you know that if a man dies with a lie on his lips, he'll go to hell for sure."

"It ain't no lie, massa."

They kept him there for several hours while the water slowly rose about him to his armpits. Still Toby refused to tell the men what they wanted to hear.

"Tell us what we want to know, nigger, or you is never going to see your family again."

"Take de chain off, please, white men! Take it off! I'll be drowned 'fore—"

"Not until you tell us what we want to know."

The tide was coming in fast. The men realized they would have to get Toby out quickly or he would drown. That they did not want. Sooner or later, they figured, he would break down and tell them where the treasure was buried. Dead, he would be no good to them.

The men started working to unfasten the chain from the root of the mangrove tree, but it was almost impossible in the deepening black water. The chain had become hopelessly tangled. There was only one way to save Toby—to yank up the root. They all worked furiously to free him for a later time. Toby pulled frantically on the chain while the others tugged at the root. The waters continued to climb. Suddenly, at the last possible moment, the root came loose, and the chains slipped away. The men hauled Toby to higher land.

Corrie told us her stories over and over again, and we never tired of hearing them.

I feel strongly that any children denied the privilege of the companionship of a black person such as Corrie in their youth have been denied one of God's greatest offerings. Her world was one of love, miracles, and sharing.

Corrie had a reason for all things. Why do trees continue to stand after they die rather than fall down? "Trees has spirits, jist like a man," she would say. "Dat's why dey stands after dey is dead. Best leave dem be."

What were those spooky sounds in the woods at night?

"When de young moon shines, all dem dat is cheated out of dere lives comes back an' walks agin."

I find it sad now to return to Monroeville. Corrie died in 1942. Jenny's big house burned down ten years later. A new one has been built on the site, but it is not the same. No one has lived there for over twenty years. Only the bone fence survives. The backyard is a jungle. The roses run wild. The orange and scarlet trumpet-vine bells sway from the top of a magnolia tree. But there is no one today to catch the perfume on the winds.

If Corrie were there today, she would say, "Chile, see de way dat trumpet vine is a-bowin' an' a-swayin' at yo? It's best to bow back."

• CHAPTER SEVEN •

The KKK Rally
and Other Adventures

THERE WAS AN AIR of tension and excitement in the big house that warm day in late April of 1930. The rooms must be swept and cleaned. The vases in every room must be filled with the King Alfred daffodils. It was spring. Truman was returning to Monroeville after spending several months with his parents. All around the porch great clusters of purple grapelike blossoms hung from the wisteria. They had not yet reached full bloom. This would offend the small boy who thought the world and the universe should be at his command. He loved the flowers and the many mingled odors in our garden.

The bus would bring Truman and his mother in from New Orleans about four o'clock in the afternoon. We all knew that Lillie Mae would not stay for long—just overnight, and then she would take the bus back to New Orleans the following afternoon to join her husband in their hotel room.

We also knew that Truman would be happy to be back in Monroeville. The Faulk home was the only home he had ever known. For him, life with his parents had meant cramped quarters in a big hotel and few companions his own age. Sook sensed that Truman would be staying with them for a longer time now. Things were not right between Arch and Lillie Mae, and she talked often of a separation, even a divorce (a scandal that no Faulk had ever fallen into before). Even though this was sad news for some, to Sook it meant the joy and possession of this sad, grown-up child of six.

167

Mr. Wiggins pulled up in his old car and dropped off Truman and Lillie Mae, after having picked them up at the bus station. Sook smoothed down her hair and ran outside, right past Lillie Mae, and cried, "Oh, my darling Tru, come inside and have a glass of tea and some lemon meringue pie. I know how exhausted you must be, you poor child."

Sook gently took Truman by his hand and led him to the kitchen. He took one look at the lemon meringue pie she had baked for him that morning and stamped his foot. "They are not tall enough," he pouted. "You know I only like lemon meringue pie when the peaks are very, very tall."

Tears welled up in Sook's eyes as she said, "Well, darling, I will just have to make another one because I want my baby to be ever so happy."

This precocious child had already mastered the art of getting those around him to cater to all his needs. Truman knew then that he had everything under control. This would be a perfect summer.

Truman changed the subject.

"Sook, I hope you have the pictures cut out and the frames made for the kites. You've had all winter to do it, you know."

Sook ran to the pantry, gathered up a great armload of colorful magazine pictures and her handmade kite frames, and put them down before Truman.

"Well, this is good," he said in his rather imperious manner. "Tomorrow we will fly kites if the wind is good."

"I hope the wind is good, Tru, because I am really not able to climb the fig tree and get your kite down."

"Oh, never mind that, Sook," Truman answered. "No wind—no kites. I promise."

Truman realized that he had to get everything understood between himself and Sook before Jenny came home from the store because then all demands would cease. She had little sympathy for Sook's willingness to spoil the boy and tolerated none of Truman's demands. If a scene developed, it usually ended with Sook sobbing in her room and Truman quietly looking on. But that previous summer when he talked Sook into ordering Tobie, the gardener, to dig all of Jenny's plants out of her large flower pit and then to fill the hole with water so that he could have a swimming pool, the day ended in tears for all.

"Sook, why are you so afraid of Jenny?" Truman once asked her.

"Darling Tru, you know she takes care of me. This is her house and her money. Never for a moment can I forget that. The only money I ever have for myself is from my dropsy medicine."

"Sook," Truman said softly, coming close to her chair and putting his arms around her frail shoulders, "don't worry. Someday I will take you away from here. Then it will be just the two of us."

"I'd like that," Sook whispered to him. "We'll go far away, maybe up in the clouds, and just sail around and watch everybody below."

Truman then made a careful tour of inspection of the big house, going from room to room, like a bird escaped from its cage. The white serge suit had to go, so he changed into a pair of khaki shorts. He wanted to shed his tan-and-white shoes, but it was too early. It was barefoot weather, but everyone knew that the official kickoff was not until May 1. Truman then went into the yard and gave a quick look around.

Nelle Harper Lee was balanced precariously on the bone fence. She waved when Truman came through the door. All afternoon she had paced back and forth in front of her house, waiting for the bus from New Orleans to arrive. When she saw Truman, Nelle immediately did a handstand. "Hey, there," she shouted. "Look what I can do."

A few minutes later Hutch, Billy Eugene, and a couple of other neighborhood children joined them in the big backyard.

Now their gang was complete. The next few days would be spent making plans for the summer. The tree house would be cleaned out and reorganized, bottles would be collected for their lightning bugs, grasshoppers, and June bugs, and magazines would be piled up to await a rainy day when, scissors in hand, they would go through looking for the right pictures to decorate their kites. Summer would soon be in full swing. Once again Truman had the security of the big white house.

Whenever the tree house became too hot and crowded, Truman and his gang moved their activities to the scuppernong grape arbor by the side of our house. There they had more space and cooler air for their playacting and storytelling.

One day in June I was sitting on the porch swing, hopelessly lost in a romantic novel, when the distraction from the arbor became too great and the book lost its interest for me. Truman was telling some of his wild tales. The kids were all goggle-eyed. Occasionally there would be an "Aw, you don't mean it." Sometimes Truman would lower his voice to a whisper when he was recounting something particularly wicked about New Orleans. Now he was telling them about a man in New Orleans, a friend of his, who kept a live tiger in his basement.

"I tell you," Truman said, "that tiger is ferocious. He has already eaten two people alive that I know about and goodness knows how many more. But he likes me. And when I pet him, he just purrs like a kitten. One day a man came to repair something in the basement, and that tiger would have swallowed him in one bite if my friend hadn't been right there."

Then Truman told them again, probably for the thousandth time, how two summers before he had sung and tap-danced on the big steamboat of the Streckfus Steamship Company where his father worked, entertaining a large crowd. They had loved him and tossed him lots of money. ("When I am old enough, I will have enough to buy my very own car!")

One moment Truman's imagination would make him a piti-ful pauper, cruelly cast into a dungeon. The next moment he would be a charming prince presiding over his court. (Years later Nelle had a lot to say about this side of Truman in her novel *To Kill a Mockingbird:* "Dill Harris [that was the name she gave Truman] could tell the biggest lies I ever heard. Among other things, he had been up in a mail plane seventeen times, he had been to Nova Scotia, he had seen an elephant, and his granddaddy was Brigadier General Joe Wheeler and left him his sword.")

The stories flowed on for some time until suddenly they stopped. All hopped out of the arbor, ran around the front of the house, and disappeared in the back.

I had just about managed to regain my interest in the novel when Truman and Nelle walked slowly up to the front porch. Nelle took a seat on the top step, propped her elbows on her knees, and clasped her face in her hands. Truman slid onto the porch swing, dangling his bare feet over the side. I continued to read my book, mindful of the pair of bright blue eyes peering into my face.

"You know, Tiny, you're the best aunt I've got," Truman said, in a low, sincere voice.

Look out! Here it comes! Silence.

"I mean it, Tiny. You've always treated me real good."

More silence. I was not about to say a thing. Finally, how-ever, my curiosity got the best of me.

"That's fine, Truman. Now what can I do for you?"

"Oh, nothing, Tiny. I just felt like telling you," he said.

I knew that there was something else. "Come on now. Tell me what you two are up to."

"Well," Truman said, drawing the word out as though it were spelled with six *e*'s and four *l*'s. "We just found out they're going to have a Ku Klux Klan meeting in the field back of the school tonight after dusk, and we wanted you to go with us to take a look."

"Oh, no, I can't do that."

"It's nothing," Truman insisted. "All we want to do is to go to the edge of the woods and take one good look. We would go by ourselves, but we thought it would be better to have a grown person along with us, and you're almost grown."

"I don't think we should, Truman," I told him. "If Jenny ever found out, she would never forgive me. And you—you would get your bottom spanked like never before."

"It's all right, Tiny. No one will ever find out, I promise. We can meet in front of the house at eight o'clock, sneak over for a good look, and then be right back home in fifteen minutes."

To tell the truth, I was a little curious myself. I had never seen a KKK rally either.

"OK," I said. "But, remember—not a word to another soul."

"Gee, thanks, Tiny," Truman said. He and Nelle both jumped up and ran around the corner of the house to where the others were waiting.

Several of us met at eight o'clock as we had planned. We cut through Mr. Broughton's yard (being careful not to disturb his ill-tempered mongrel) and then made our way across a barbed-wire fence, through a field to the edge of the woods. I cautioned the kids to be very quiet. We hid in the shadows and peered down into the open field on the other side of the patch of woods.

We saw a large group of white-hooded figures milling around. Several carried crosses in their hands. Three big bonfires burned brightly, casting eerie shadows over the entire scene. One of the men was addressing the others, but we were too far away to hear his words.

"That's Mr. Plunk," Truman whispered excitedly, pointing toward the man who was speaking. "I swear that's Mr. Plunk."

"Shut up, you idiot," Nelle said, slapping her hand across his mouth.

"I want a better look," Truman announced. He climbed up a small tree nearby and crawled out on a limb. Suddenly, the limb broke with a sharp crack, which sounded like a pistol shot in the still night. Truman plopped to the ground like a sack of oats. "Help me, help me!" he shouted at the top of his lungs. In the field beyond all the talking stopped. The hooded men looked intently in our direction. Three creatures bearing torches started toward us. One of them carried a rifle.

"Run," Truman hollered. "Run for your lives."

We all flew past the woods, through the open field, to the barbed-wire fence beyond. The other kids scrambled under the fence. Truman spread the two strands and crawled between, but before he could get safely through, the barbed wires snapped back into place right onto his bottom.

"Wait," he pleaded. "I'm stuck. Please don't leave me."

Nelle wheeled around and gave the wire a strong jerk. Truman was freed.

"Good Lord," he cried, and then ran on, leaving behind on the barbed wire some skin and a big piece of his pants.

We came through the lot around the corner and then split up, each heading toward home.

Truman crab-walked into the living room where Jenny was reading.

"Where have you been?" she asked. "Why, Truman, you look like you have just seen a ghost."

"Oh, just outside," he replied. But he knew that she had spoken some truth.

"Bud," Truman said one morning, "I've been thinking. Billy

and Nanny haven't been baptized. I'd like to take them down to Hatter's Pond and get them saved. Will you help me?"

Bud thought for a moment, holding back a chuckle. Truman was referring to two goats he had adopted as his pets. "Sure, Truman," he finally said. "If you want your goats saved, I'll help you."

Bud helped Truman tie the ropes around the neck of each. "You lead Nanny, and I'll take Billy," he suggested.

Down the dusty lane they went, Nanny trotting along peacefully while Billy held back to nibble at the grass along the side of the road. Finally, they all arrived at the edge of Hatter's Pond. Bud held Nanny while Truman led Billy into the dark brown waters. She was ready to be saved and offered up no resistance. Truman pushed her head under the water, saying solemnly, "You are saved." Then he came ashore to get Billy and marched him into the pond until only his head showed above the water. Truman pulled at his horns, trying to force him completely under, but Billy would have no part of this ceremony. Truman tugged, fought, and jerked, all to no avail. Finally, he lost all his patience and shouted, "All right, you damn billy goat. You're going to hell anyway, so go on and go to hell!"

Truman that day provided Bud with one of his favorite stories. Each time he told it, he embroidered it slightly. When he came to the punch line, he would slap his knee and laugh uproariously.

Truman's favorite pet was Queenie, a black-and-white-spotted rat terrier, who became his inseparable companion for many of those years in Monroeville. Queenie came to us late one night in the autumn. A nasty cold rain had fallen most of the evening. Truman was out on the back porch when he suddenly spotted a very wet and very miserable puppy curled up in the ray of light coming through the kitchen window. He carefully wrapped the shivering dog in a blanket and carried him to his bedroom, where he hid him for several days, feeding him scraps he managed to scavenge from the kitchen. But then Jenny, hearing strange noises, investigated and found the dog. She was not happy. Jenny had no use for pets of any sort around her home, especially dogs. But Truman was adamant. He swore up and down that he would take care of the puppy so that he would never bother anyone. Jenny finally relented.

The strange part was that Queenie was a male dog. One day soon after the puppy was established as the newest member of the household, Bud asked Truman, "What are you going to name your dog?"

"His name is Queenie," Truman replied.

"No, Truman," Bud persisted, "you can't call him Queenie. That's a girl's name. You will have to name him Spot or Rover or something like that."

"The dog's name is Queenie, and that's all there is to it," Truman insisted emphatically. And that settled that.

Queenie continued as an integral part of our household long after Truman left Monroeville. Finally, years later, he was killed, kicked in the head by a neighbor's horse. "I wrapped Queenie in a fine linen sheet and rode him in your old baby buggy down to Simpson's pasture where he can be with all his bones," Sook wrote Truman, who was by then far away in New York City.

When Truman came of age, Jenny enrolled him in the Monroe County Grammar School. From the start he disliked school and used any excuse he could find to stay home. He lied shamelessly and feigned one illness after another. Truman was a great little actor. His asthma attacks looked so real that Sook was always ready to send him in an ambulance to Mobile. Truman loved the afternoon soap operas that were broadcast over the radio. He and Sook would sit in the kitchen and listen to them by the hour. After three days of an imagined cold, Truman would get all involved with "The Goldbergs," "One Man's Family," and "Just Plain Bill." Then it would be torture for him to go back to school and not know what was happening to his favorite characters.

Jenny always made certain that Truman went off to school neatly dressed with polished Buster Brown shoes on his feet. No child from her house would show up at school in bare feet!

I remember one particular morning when Jenny was in the front yard cutting and replanting some japonica bushes and gathering some rose blooms for the store. She always cut her roses in the early morning when they still had dew on their petals.

Truman came out of the house and tried to get by Jenny unobserved. He had his shoes off, shoelaces tied together, and slung over his shoulder. Now he could eat the boiled peanuts he had stuffed into his pockets and step into every mud puddle on his way to school.

"Now don't that beat all," Jenny said to Corrie, who had come onto the porch. "I spend a lot of my hard-earned money to buy that boy a fine pair of shoes, and he can't wait to get them off his feet and walk barefoot through cow paddies and Lord knows what else."

"Well, don't yo fret you'self none, Miz Jenny, 'cause when he goes by de Boular hus he's goin' be flyin'."

Our house was only four down from the corner where Truman turned to head toward school. Next door was the Lee house, then the Hendrix house, and finally the Boular house. The schoolyard adjoined the Boular house, and many of the children had to pass it in order to get to school. It never failed to give them the shudders. At night the kids cut across to the opposite side of the street rather than walk alongside the Boular property.

The Boular house was a desolate and mournful place, no doubt of that. The shades were always pulled down, and there never seemed to be any good times inside. The yard was dark and foreboding; the old oak trees kept the sunlight out. No one ever put in time on the yard. Johnson grass and rabbit tobacco grew there in abundance. Surrounding it all was one of those tall, heavily ornamental black iron fences that would have been much more at home in a cemetery than around a yard.

The Boular family had for years had an air of mystery hanging over them. Mr. Boular was a tall, thin man with a long face and high cheekbones. He had a bad stutter, which is why he never said a word to you when he passed you on the street but just touched his hand to the brim of his hat. He ran the feed store in town. His wife was a small woman with pale blue eyes and lashless lids that blinked constantly as though she had a particle of clay dust perpetually caught underneath.

The Boulars had three children, a son and two daughters. One daughter married and moved out of town. The other met with tragedy while vacationing on the Gulf of Mexico. It was a ghastly death, and we would tell the story over and over again on moonless nights when we wanted to get ourselves really frightened. The girl's name was Lollie, and she had gone to Bayou La Batre on the corner of Mobile Bay for a weekend with some friends from Mobile. She and several other young people were all splashing around in a swimming hole on a river. Suddenly, Lollie started struggling and screaming. She tried desperately to wade ashore. The other swimmers saw to their horror that a giant alligator had grabbed her right leg and was slowly dragging her into deeper water. The women shrieked hysterically. The men stood mesmerized in knee-deep water, watching as the poor girl was pulled farther and farther from the shore. Finally, Lollie's head and arms disappeared beneath the surface. No trace of her body was ever found.

The son was about my age. We called him Caw because he had a habit of making strange noises that sounded like the cawing of a crow.

The most frightening thing about Caw was his eyes. They were the most unnatural eyes I have ever seen, huge and round like a newborn baby's. They never seemed to blink but only to peer at you with a vacant stare. Caw had a scary way of suddenly leaning over the top of the fence as you walked by and whispering vague mutterings out of the side of his mouth as you passed. He was clearly not all there in the head. The townspeople treated him like a joke or some sort of animal most of the time. The children were all frightened of him. He scooted in and out of the heavy leaves of the magnolia tree in his yard like some desperate monkey. Caw would sometimes fly into violent rages, and there were rumors that once he had tried to strangle his own father—in fact, would have done it had not his mother come in at the last minute.

The Boular house was spooky all right. Years later Nelle would take it over with some changes and put it into her novel *To Kill A Mockingbird* as the "Radley place." And Caw would become Boo Radley, who would play such an important part in the ending of that book.

Truman soon began to bring home stories about Caw Boular. One day he reported that Caw had come up to the fence as he had walked by and said, "Aren't you the littlest fellow I've ever seen. Don't go away. Come on back." Another time Caw had reached through the bars of the fence and tried to grab Truman's leg as he walked by.

Jenny wanted to know more details.

"He told me to take my books home and then come right back or I would be sorry. I'd be the sorriest kid in the graveyard. Those were his words, Jenny. Then a funny thing happened. He changed and said, 'Don't be afraid. I won't hurt you. Please come back. Please . . .' But I didn't. I don't want ever to talk to him again. I'm scared of him."

"Dat pore Boular family," Corrie put in. "Dat Caw is 'bout

as mean as a rattlesnake in a corner. Youse watch you'self, Truman."

"Now, Truman, you just stay away from him and you'll be all right. I swear, I just don't know why that father of his doesn't commit that boy to an institution and be done with it. He has been more trouble to them than a barrel full of mice."

"Why is he that way?" Truman wanted to know. Even as a child he had a morbid curiosity about the outcasts of society, especially if there was some sort of ghoulish mystery involved.

"Truman, I wish I knew," said Jenny. "That poor boy has been shut up and shunned like he was some sort of polecat ever since he was a little one. Caw has always been a strange one. I remember a few years ago when he killed old Mrs. Bussey's black cat, Robert E. Lee, cut him open, stuffed him with rocks, and then put him in the hole in that old chinaberry tree that sits right in the middle of the fork in the road. What a commotion that made. I think everybody in town must have come by to see that cat."

"Dat ain't all, Miz Jenny," Corrie put in excitedly. "Tell dat chile 'bout de time Caw done tried to choke his own daddy!"

"Tell it! Tell it!" Truman shouted. He was beside himself with anticipation.

"Quiet down, child. That's just a story. No one knows for certain what happened."

"But, Jenny, I want to hear it, please. What happened?"

"Well, Truman," Jenny began, "it seems that late one summer evening five years ago Mr. Boular was sitting in his swing, swinging back and forth as peacefully as could be. Suddenly, Mrs. Boular heard the squeaking of the swing stop. After a few minutes she called to her husband, but no answer came back. When Mrs. Boular went to investigate, she found him unconscious on the swing, a piece of wisteria vine knotted tightly around his neck. His face was all blue, and his eyes looked like they were ready to pop out of his head. For a week afterward Mr. Boular went about town with a white cloth tied loosely around his neck. That's when people started saying that Caw had tried to strangle his own father. Of course, it may just be a story with no truth to it. I can't say."

When Jenny finished her story, Truman sat there for the longest time, not moving, hardly even breathing.

"Oh, Jenny," he finally whispered, "of course Caw did it. I just know he did. And just think—Caw almost had me, too. What a close call that was!"

One time Jenny decided that it would be a good idea to let Truman, who was then six, invite several of his friends to attend a Chautauqua on the outskirts of Mobile. He would forget about his mother and father, who had recently decided upon a divorce. She put the whole group up overnight at the famous Battlehouse Hotel where the blood-red carpet was ankle deep.

I went along as the kids' chaperone. Once we got to the Chautauqua, all the kids wanted to see the freak show first. A stone-faced man with a cigar in the corner of his mouth and dark brown juice running down his chin was hawking the sights within.

"Shocking, sensational, sexational. Ladies and gentlemen, step right up for the show of your life."

The way it worked was that you went inside and then paid a small fee to see each exhibit. The kids strolled by one tent after another until they came to one with a big banner over the entrance that read simply "HERMAPHRODITE." They stopped dead in their tracks.

"What's a hermaphrodite, Tiny?" Truman wanted to know.

"Well, Truman," I told him, "it's sort of a cross between a man and a woman. But I think you all will probably enjoy the six-legged cow more. Why don't we visit that tent?"

But no, Truman wanted to see the hermaphrodite. He

stepped up to the platform outside where another hawker was extolling the wonder within.

"Come on in, it's a gen-u-ine hermaphrodite, the most amazing wonder known to medical science. He's a she and will show you the works. Only one slim dime gets you in."

Just as the barker was about to launch into another spiel, he spied Truman looking up at him. "Pretty boy," he said, "beat it. You're not old enough for this here show."

I bought us all tickets. I had my reservations, of course, but I was as curious as they were about what a hermaphrodite looked like. I figured Jenny would never find out about it.

As we entered the tent, we saw inside a sagging platform decorated with a fringed lamp and a somewhat soiled gold chair. On it sat a bizarre and epicene creature with large brown eyes, heavily lidded like those of a hawk. Its fiery red hair was carefully curled and piled high on its head. The creature was dressed in a long flowing robe of cheap gold silk. Its hands were heavily weighted down with costume jewelry. Slowly it opened its robe. Its skin was pure white with a cadaverous look about it. It exposed partially developed breasts and seductively caressed one of its nipples. I remember that they were red and so big that they looked like young apples.

Spellbound, we simply stood there without saying a word. Then the creature shifted its position and opened the robe again, this time from the middle. Slowly, teasingly, it drew apart the gold folds. Finally, it exposed a red V of bushy hair wedged between crossed legs. Then with a lewd smile the creature parted its legs and with its jeweled fingers reached between its thighs into the clump of hair to extract a small white fleshy growth. It pulled it out about as far as flesh can be stretched and then devilishly waved the flap at the small crowd in front. Finally, it tucked it back between its legs and covered itself once again. And that was the end of the act.

One of the most memorable people in Monroeville was Meyer Katz, the head of our town's only Jewish family. Mr. Katz had been born in Kiev, Russia, and had emigrated to the United States in 1905. Two years later he brought over his wife and children. During his early years in the South, he traveled by foot from town to town, selling merchandise from a pack sack. Later he bought a horse and buggy. In 1914 Mr. Katz settled in Monroeville and opened a store on the town square opposite Jenny's shop. He carried clothing, home furnishings, and white goods. Mr. Katz's big item was shoes. Jenny never carried shoes because, she said, she would have no part of smelly feet. So she sent her customers who wanted shoes over to Mr. Katz's shop. The two of them had great admiration for each other.

You always read about how hard it was for Jews to live in the Deep South for much of this century. I suppose it was true elsewhere, but not in Monroeville. Mr. Katz was highly regarded by just about everyone, and nobody ever really thought twice about the fact that his was the town's only Jewish family. In fact, David, one of his sons, told me recently that once he and two of his brothers, all of whom were accomplished musicians, had even played at a Ku Klux Klan rally, more as a joke than anything else, I suppose. But there you have it.

There was a large open space behind Mr. Katz's store (years before my father had had his horse stable there) that became popular for fistfights, cockfights, card games—anything slightly illegal or immoral. One day a boy even brought a small alligator to wrestle. In the summer, on a Saturday afternoon when everybody came into town with wives and children to shop and socialize, there was always something going on behind Mr. Katz's store.

One afternoon in the summer of 1930 I took Truman and Nelle to that lot behind Mr. Katz's store to see a snake fight. Some crazy old man from the bayou country had brought the snakes into town for that purpose. Nelle had first gotten wind of it. None of us had ever heard of such a thing before. So off we went. Jenny, of course, knew nothing about it.

A big dry-goods box held the two snakes, a water moccasin and a king snake. Neither of the snakes appeared much interested in the other. Each lay neatly coiled with its head pillowed on its body in an attitude of vigilant repose. About twenty-five people crowded around the box, each of whom had paid a dime to see the fight. There was quite a bit of betting on one snake or the other. I seem to recall that the water moccasin was the favorite.

For the longest time we all stood there, waiting for one of the snakes to make a move. Neither did. Then finally the moccasin twitched its tail and began slowly to shift its position along one side of the box. The king snake raised its head and slowly swung it back and forth like a pendulum. Both snakes looked long and hard at each other, flicking their red tongues out rapidly. They held their positions for a long time. It didn't look as though anything would happen. Then suddenly someone sounded the horn of an automobile parked nearby. That startled everybody, including the snakes. They leaped, and the next thing we knew they were wrapped around each other. They were so tangled up that we could not tell which had which. Finally the king snake appeared to get the upper hand, wrapping itself methodically around the moccasin tighter and tighter. After a long time we heard a muffled snap, like a dry twig being broken. The moccasin lashed its tail a few times and then lay still. I couldn't wait to get out of there with Truman and Nelle. I was afraid Jenny would suddenly appear to check out the noise and see us all there.

One day in July 1931 I sat on our porch swing reading an article on John Gilbert in a recent issue of *Liberty*. Truman gathered up Jenny's copy of *Webster's Dictionary*, which he was memorizing, and went out to sit by the old yellow rosebush. As if by some telepathy, over the bone fence, kerplop, came Nelle. I decided this would be the ideal time for me to slip off and do some shopping in town. I suspected that Truman and Nelle would be busy with that dictionary for quite a spell. The bigger the word, the more fascinating it would be for those two.

I quietly got up from the swing and walked through the house, out the back door, and down the driveway. After passing three houses I looked back, and there were Truman and Nelle following stealthily behind, slightly crouched, almost on tiptoes, furtively gaining ground. The hot, powdery clay packed between their toes, then flew upward in pinkish puffs with each step.

I stopped, No use to go on that way.

"For Pete's sake, Truman, you and Nelle come on if you are determined to go with me. It's hot, you know, so let's not dawdle."

Within seconds the two of them were at my side, breathless and looking somewhat guilty. The sixty cents in my pocket for a soda and a magazine would now buy three sodas instead.

"Truman, I swear, can't I ever do anything without you and Nelle along?"

"Do anything without us?" Truman quipped. "What on earth are you talking about? We decided to go to town, that's all. Just because you happened to be going too doesn't mean we are following you."

"Well," I said, "you know and I know you are following me."

"Maybe so," admitted Truman. "That's not important. The important thing is—do you have any money? I'm thirsty. Let's go to the drugstore and get a huge soda. Surely you have that much money. You know very well that if I had the money I would treat you."

"All right, all right, just hush," I said. "I have only sixty cents, so that will buy us each a soda."

"Tell you what," Truman said. "Let's charge the sodas at the drugstore because I want to buy Sook a present, and besides, I want a pearl-handled knife."

When we reached the square, Truman and Nelle stepped lightly on the paved sidewalks, for the heat was intense. Occasionally Truman would step over into the dirt street and dance a few steps of the Charleston to cool the bottoms of his feet in the warm dust. The streets were about empty, for only a few braved the heat. There was only a small group of kids gathered around the courthouse stoop.

"Look," Truman shouted. "They're frying eggs on the courthouse steps."

"Let's go over and watch," put in Nelle.

"No, indeed," I said. "It's just too hot. Let's do what we have to do and then go home. We'll go to Monroe Drugs first and cool off."

We walked into the empty drugstore and gave a sigh of relief. Ralph was behind the counter and greeted us as we came in.

"Hi, Tiny. Hi, Truman. Hi, Nelle."

Ralph was my age, and we had gone through school together. Truman picked a table under the big fan in the center of the room. The long blades whirled around, making a grinding sound, stirring up the hot air. Ralph came over and wiped off our table.

"How come you didn't get to Snook's party last night, Tiny?" he wanted to know. "Everybody was there but you. Somebody said you went to New Orleans."

"I was supposed to go to New Orleans but had a change of plans at the last moment," I replied.

"Carol Anne is having a party Friday night, and I sure hope you'll be there. It'll be a good one. Did she call you?"

"She called this morning, and I'll be there," I promised.

Ralph had wiped the table until the surface shone. "Now, what will you three have?" he asked.

Truman spoke up first. "I'll have a fluffy soda, make it strawberry, and put in an extra scoop of ice cream, and make it extra fluffy."

"I'll have the same," Nelle said.

"Ralph, just bring me a cherry Coke," I said.

Ralph left to prepare the drinks.

Truman turned to me and mimicked: "'How come you didn't get to Snook's party last night?' Hey, Tiny, I think he's sweet on you."

Nelle snickered.

Mr. Yarborough, the druggist, popped out from the back to check on things. He stayed only a second and then retreated to the rear of the store once again.

"Would you like me to give you a description of Mr. Yarborough?" Truman asked us, and then, without waiting for an answer, he continued. "Horned hair, snake eyes, snoopy nose, jagged teeth, peaked ears, beany arms, round bottom, and stilt legs," he announced proudly.

I thought about it for a minute and then realized that he really had described Mr. Yarborough perfectly. At that moment Ralph brought over our drinks, and we started sipping them under the cool of the fan.

"Now, Truman, I have only sixty cents with me, and that will just about cover the cost of these drinks, unless we charge them to Jenny. What else was it that you wanted to buy today?"

"I want to get something for Sook's birthday," Truman answered, "but I can't remember when it is. Do you know?"

I thought about it for a while but couldn't remember. As far as I knew, Sook had never had a birthday. At least, she never had a birthday party. Everyone else had birthday parties, but never Sook. That could only mean she didn't want people to know. "Truman, I honestly do not know," I told him.

"Isn't it strange," he said, "that she makes so much fuss over everybody's else's birthday, but she won't let anybody know about her own? I am going to buy her something anyway. We'll all go to Dr. Fripp's store and I'll pick out something extra-special nice for her."

We finished our drinks, and I charged them to Jenny on our way out.

"'Bye, Tiny. 'Bye, Truman. 'Bye, Nelle," Ralph called as we went out the front door.

Truman didn't even bother to mimic him. He was much too intent on what he would buy Sook.

We walked over to Dr. Fripp's general-goods store. He greeted us as last-minute saviors.

"Come right in," he said. "What may I show you?"

"I just want to look around," Truman said.

"I've got some new toys in," Dr. Fripp said. "I think you will like them. Let me show you them."

"No, thanks," Truman replied, "I just want to look around."

Truman went from counter to counter, examining article after article, but he always came back to the egg beaters. He picked up several and gave each one a gentle twirl.

"I'll take this one," he finally decided, and handed the egg beater to Dr. Fripp.

"Please wrap it in white tissue paper and tie it off with a red ribbon and a big bow."

Dr. Fripp looked a little astonished but did as he was commanded. Then he asked, "Wouldn't you like a little something for yourself?"

"I'll look at some knives," Truman said.

Dr. Fripp pulled out a large tray of pocket knives. Truman examined them closely, snapping several of the blades.

"Haven't you got a pearl-handled knife?" Truman asked.

"No, Truman," Dr. Fripp answered. "But all the boys want this Boy Scout knife with the three blades."

"No, thank you," said Truman. "I want it for Bud, and I think he would like a pearl-handled knife."

"Can't I show you some toys or something for yourself?" Dr. Fripp persisted.

"No, thanks," Truman said. "I'll just take the egg beater. How much is it?"

"It's twenty-five cents," Dr. Fripp replied. "But never mind. I'll just charge it to Miss Jenny."

"No," Truman said, "that won't be right. This is a present and I will have to pay for it myself."

He pulled a dollar bill out of his pocket (goodness knows where it came from) and took the change.

The three of us then walked over to Jenny's store. She was in the back talking to Mrs. Scarbath. We walked to where they were, so that we could enjoy the blast from the elctric fan.

"I declare, Truman," Mrs. Scarbath exclaimed. "You look just like your mother did at your age. You're just too pretty to be a boy." She reached over to give Truman an embrace, but he shrank back.

"I have to be going now, Jenny," Mrs. Scarbath said. "Give me a call when the new merchandise comes in." She strutted out of the store as if she owned it.

"I just hate that woman," Truman said. "She is the most insincere person I've known in my entire life."

"Don't say that, Truman," Jenny insisted. "She is my best customer, and I expect you to be civil to her. Now what is that package you've got under your arm?"

"This is just something I bought myself for Sook," Truman said. "It's nothing."

"Well, young man, it had better not be anything you've charged to me. I swear, you kids are charging things all over town to me, and I mean to put a stop to it."

This was one of Jenny's most common complaints, but we all knew she would never put a stop to it. Actually to do so would be to humble herself in the eyes of the townspeople, and that is something Jenny's pride would never permit.

Another customer came into the store, and Jenny became so busy that the three of us left and went home.

Sook was in the kitchen making blackberry pies.

"There you are, Tru," she said. "You told me you were going to help me with these pies. But never you mind."

Truman pulled out his package that he had hidden behind his back and handed it to Sook. "This is for your birthday, whenever it is," he told her.

Sook grabbed the package with eager delight, carefully untying the ribbon and unfolding the tissue paper. She danced with joy when she saw what Truman had bought her and then cautiously placed the shiny egg beater in the kitchen cabinet and gave Truman a big hug. This time Truman did not shrink back.

"Oh, thank you, darling Tru," she said. "I am so happy. Now we will have meringue a foot tall!"

The next trip to Mobile he brought back a pearl-handled knife for Bud.

Truman's closest friend in his Monroeville years was Nelle Harper Lee who lived next door to us. They were constant companions and always into mischief together. The pair of them together probably flew more kites, played more games of jacks, shot more marbles, shinned up more trees, and helped build more tree houses than any other two authors in the world. When Truman wrote his first novel, *Other Voices, Other Rooms*, he put Nelle in as the tomboy Idabel. Nelle's character Dill Harris in *To Kill a Mockingbird* is a faithful portrait of the young Truman.

Nelle, born in Monroeville on April 28, 1926, is two years younger than Truman. Although both shared the same rich texture of life in a small Southern town, Nelle had the added benefit of parents who were loving and caring toward her. Her father, Amasa Coleman Lee, was born in Georgiana, Alabama, in 1880. In 1913 he came to Monroeville and went to work as a legal apprentice in the law firm of Barnett and Bugg. Two years later Mr. Lee was admitted to the bar, and in 1916 he became a partner with Barnett and Bugg. From 1929 to 1947 he served as the editor of our local weekly newspaper, The *Monroeville Journal*.

The portrait of Atticus Finch in *To Kill a Mockingbird* is an idealization of Nelle's father. (There never was any such trial, by the way, at least not in Monroeville, and Mr. Lee never handled any cases that were remotely like that.) Mr. Lee was a tall, angular man, detached, not particularly friendly, especially with children. In fact, most of us kids were quite intimidated by him and his rather formal ways. He was not the sort of father who came up to his children, ruffled their hair, and made jokes for their amusement. Nelle today is the spitting image of her father with his square, angular face, strong, thin mouth, dark eyes, heavy eyebrows, and black hair. (Years later she gave Gregory Peck her father's gold watch at the completion of the filming of *To Kill a Mockingbird*.)

Frances, or Miss Fanny as we called her, was Nelle's mother. She came from a fine old Virginia family. She was an accomplished pianist and spent much of each day playing classical compositions. Miss Fanny never cared much for domestic responsibilities, leaving those to Haddy, their live-in Negro servant. She was a good mother, kind to her children. She was a big woman, but you were never conscious of her bulk. She carried herself with considerable grace and elegance. Miss Fanny always wore her gorgeous platinum-blond hair in two thick braids that she coiled around on the top of her head.

The Lee home was a white-frame one-story bungalow with a porch that went the length of the front. Fig trees, crape myrtles, and pecan trees grew in pleasing confusion in the yard. Miss Fanny rarely had any domestic duties to perform and took little interest in the house, especially its furnishings. The house was comfortable but sparsely furnished with wooden chairs, iron bedsteads, and floors of highly polished pine with no rugs. Miss Fanny's chief responsibility around the house appeared to be tending the flower boxes that were filled with petunias, which flowered throughout the summer. In some ways she was very much a creature of habit. If we saw Miss Fanny watering her plants, we knew it was ten o'clock in the morning. When she finished, she would disappear inside, and a few minutes later we would hear the first strains of Debussy or Chopin as she sat down at her piano. Miss Fanny rarely altered her morning routine.

The Lees had four children. A son died shortly after birth. The first daughter, Alice, was my age and her father's favorite. She was as smart as could be and studied law at Huntington College in Montgomery. (We were roommates there together.) She followed in her father's footsteps and took over his practice in Monroeville, which she still runs today from her office in the old courthouse. Alice never married.

Louise, the second daughter, was rather prim and proper, the exact opposite of Nelle, who grew up a high-strung, boisterous, noisy tomboy. She much preferred overalls to dresses. In fact, a dress on the young Nelle would have been as out of place as a silk hat on a hog's head. She was a real fighter and could lick most of the boys her age in town. Truman learned quickly never to get into a quarrel with Nelle. She always ended up flinging him to the ground and hopping up and down on him like an angry bantam rooster. (Nelle, by the way, is Ellen spelled backward. She was named after her maternal grandmother.)

Truman did not spend much time in Nelle's house; she always came to our place. The Lee house was different, much more subdued. Miss Fanny was not the sort of woman to encourage a gang of kids to horse around her house. Truman and Nelle had much more freedom at our place. Jenny was away during the day. There was always something to eat. She and Truman loved to walk along the top of the bone fence or play in the tree house out back.

When you heard Corrie holler, "Dere goes Miss Frippy-britches," and Nelle call out, "Hello, Truman, you little chick-en-breasted runt," you knew the two of them were together again in the yard. When they were not in their tree house with its collection of old magazines and glass jars full of grasshoppers and butterflies, the chances were they would be under the big yellow rosebushes in the backyard with an ancient Underwood typewriter that Mr. Lee had given them. They loved to play at being writers. Nelle would drag the big Underwood over. Truman would bring his tattered copy of *Webster's Dictionary*. Together they would sit for hours, pecking away.

The two of them would spend hours in Jenny's attic poring through the stacks of magazines that Sook kept there, looking for colorful pictures to paste on their kites. They especially liked *Ladies' Home Journal* because of its colorful advertisements. They could never let a Colgate Fab ad, with all its colored bubbles, go by unscissored. (As Sook said, "It's so suited for flying!") Other favorites were the Chesapeake and Ohio Railroad ads with their Chessie Cat figures.

Periodically, down below we would hear the quiet of the house suddenly shattered by loud voices.

"We've got a million of those old Fairy Soap ads, dummy," Nelle would shout. Then there would be the sound of pages being torn to bits.

"Stop that, Nelle," Truman would cry plaintively in his high-pitched voice. "Keep your hands off *my* pictures. I hate you, Nelle. I really do."

"You shut up, you silly little shrimp," Nelle would holler back, "or I'll knock your silly block off. Anyhow, you wouldn't let me cut out the stocking ad in the *Woman's Home Companion* with the black witch riding a broom. I wanted it!"

"You're crazy, Nelle. Who wants a picture of a witch on his kite? Unless, of course, the person flying the kite is one herself."

Nelle's voice would come back, loud and clear. "You watch yourself, loony bird, or you are in serious trouble."

And then nothing more would be said. Later we might see three kites flying at once—Truman's, Nelle's, and Sook's. When one of their kites got into trouble, hooked on the top of a tree, it was always Sook's job to get it down. She never allowed Truman or Nelle to climb up, fearful they might fall down.

I can still see Sook in her calico dress covered by a starched white apron with big pockets raise her hem and painfully climb a fig or pecan tree to retrieve a stranded kite.

Truman and Nelle would stand below and shout directions.

"You got to go farther out on the limb, Sook," Nelle would holler.

"Hurry up, Sook, before the wind dies down," Truman would order.

"Shucks, I'm no mockingbird," Sook would call down. "And don't you kids forget it!"

Two other favorite pastimes were marbles and jacks. The pair of them got along reasonably well when playing jacks. But when it came to marbles, they always fought over who got the aggie. Nelle usually beat Truman playing marbles because she would get right down on the ground, line up the two marbles smartly, and shoot hard. Truman, on the other hand, outplayed Nelle at jacks because his hands were more agile than hers.

In late August when the local farmers harvested their crops of peanuts, Truman and Nelle would get ready for their Saturday afternoon sales of boiled peanuts and freshly made lemonade at a little sidewalk stand they would set up. Bud always brought them several sacks of immature peanuts from his farm, which Sook then boiled in their hulls in salty water according to an old recipe that dated back to her days on the Faulk plantation. Truman and Nelle never made more than a few nickels on their "sales." They were poor businessmen, much too quick to eat their own goods rather than wait for the occasional customer.

Truman was pretty much the leader of his little circle of friends. In the long run his wild imagination and unbridled energy more than made up for his small size. I remember the summer of 1931 when Nelle, Doofie—that was Sylvester's grandson—and Twiggs Butts gathered in our yard, waiting for Truman, who was then almost seven. Suddenly Truman burst in among them, so excited that I thought he would pop a blood vessel.

"My God, y'all hear about the awful thing that happened to Mrs. Ida Skutt?" he shouted. "It was terrible, just terrible."

Nelle was practically shouting, "Who? What? Where?"

Truman was holding a melting ice-cream cone in one hand.

"Nelle, it will freeze the blood in your veins," he said between licks.

"Tell us, tell us!" the other children shouted.

"Well, this morning when the egg man left that old Mrs. Skutt a carton of eggs, he smelled an awful stink. He figured it must be one of her dead cats. And then when he came back that afternoon to collect, well, the stink was enough to kill a person. That egg man peeped through the front parlor window between the curtains. And there she was!"

"Was what, damn you?" the other kids shouted.

"*Dead! Dead! Dead!*" Truman gasped.

He waited for the full shock of his announcement to sink in. And then he lowered his voice.

"Mrs. Skutt was sitting straight up in a wing chair, dead as a fish out of water. She had been dead for days."

"Was she murdered?" one of the kids asked.

"Could be," Truman answered, "but the sheriff thinks she had a stroke or something."

"Eek," said Nelle. "Go on!"

"Well," said Truman, looking his ice-cream cone over carefully and licking the sides smooth, "there she was in her old flowered tow-sack dress with her legs spread apart so you could see her homespun drawers. Why, you could even read 'Lilly White Flour' still printed on them."

Truman took several more licks from his ice cream, all the time enjoying the effect the suspense had on the other children.

"But you know what was worse?" he finally asked. "She was alive with shiny black cockroaches. Hundreds of them. They ran up and down her legs and across her lap and crawled on her face and into her mouth. God, it was a horror to behold."

Of course, Truman had never seen the dreadful sight. He had just heard the story from Jenny and then let his imagination elaborate on the details.

"Balls of fire!" Doofie exclaimed. "Why, this is better than the day Twit Tutwiler was split open by lightnin'."

Now that Truman's melodramatic moment of excitement had passed, he was ready for other things. Doffie and Twiggs headed home. Truman and Nelle retreated to their secret hiding place beneath the yellow rosebushes. Snatches of their conversation drifted into the house.

"Say, Truman, which one of your parents do you like the best?" It was Nelle's voice.

"Well, I suppose, I really can't say," Truman offered. "They both exasperate me. I suppose I would say I am fondest of the one I'm not with at the time."

"Truman, will you marry me when we grow up?"

A few minutes later the two emerged from their sanctuary, locked their moist, dirty fingers together, and ran off, laughing.

CHAPTER EIGHT

Changes

ARCH SPENT MOST OF THE YEAR in New Orleans working for the Streckfus Steamship Company, but that work was seasonal, and he had off many of the winter months. All of us in Jenny's house knew that when December came around, Arch was sure to follow. He always made Monroeville the base for his winter operations. For the first few days Arch would settle back on the old-fashioned swing on our front porch and make himself comfortable. His eyes behind those thick-lensed glasses would slowly close until they were narrow slits. But Arch was not asleep. No, he had turned his imagination loose to chase down some foolproof scheme that would make him a pile of money in a short time with little effort. We never knew what crazy idea he might latch onto next.

I remember one rainy afternoon on a Sunday in mid-January of 1927. In Monroeville on a rainy Sunday afternoon there wasn't much to do then but rock on a front porch. Bud and Truman were in the swing at the end of the porch. Truman's legs stuck out from the swing like two small sticks. Lillie Mae, Jenny, and I all sat in rocking chairs.

Suddenly, Arch's big black Packard roared down our street. Behind the wheel was the biggest man any of us had ever seen. The Packard screeched to a halt in a rain puddle in front of our gate. Arch sat in the car while his driver slowly emerged and opened a black umbrella, which he carefully held over Arch's head as the pair walked toward our porch.

"Good afternoon, Miss Jenny and all," Arch said with a grin like the Cheshire Cat's, twirling his panama hat in his hand. "Let me introduce Sam—Sam Impastato. I am going to make him the world's next heavyweight boxing champion."

Sam Impastato was not only the biggest hunk of man I had ever met. He was the least good-looking, too. He had no hair whatsoever on his head, a curious bony ridge down the top of his skull, and huge ears that made him look like an elephant. Sam carried about 260 pounds on his six-foot two-inch frame, and all of it was muscle that had been developed to the point where his body was a parody of a normal man's.

That evening Sam informed us he had been born in a small town in Sicily and had attended the University of Rome. Arch had discovered him at Spring Hill College in Mobile, where he worked as the director of the school's physical-education program. Arch had taken one look and decided that with the proper training Sam was a sure thing for a big win on the boxing circuit. He gave the poor man one of his fast talks, persuaded him to quit his job at the college, and brought him to Monroeville to train for the big fight with Arch as his manager.

The entire scheme sounded outrageously improbable to all of us, but Jenny let the pair stay on and put Sam in a spare bedroom at the extreme left-hand corner of the porch. He even had his own private entrance. Because there was no gym in Monroeville, Arch had bought in Mobile a trunk full of exercise equipment—barbells, arm pulleys, everything that Sam needed to start his training. All this equipment went into Sam's room, which served both as a training area and a bedroom.

Every morning about six Arch would rouse Sam and take him jogging. Sam did all the work, of course. Arch would never have wasted his breath running around the town. He hired another driver, and the two of them would ride along in the Packard. Sam would be up front, jogging along, the big Packard following closely on his heels. Whenever Sam slowed down,

Arch would lean over, hit the horn, and tell the driver to step on it. That was the way it was every morning—Sam jogging along, the sweat pouring from his body, the black Packard playing bumper tag with his heels, and Arch leaning out the side window, shouting, "Don't be lazy, you damn dago, not if you want to be a world champion."

After a while Arch decided to expropriate our living room for a training center. He ordered Sam to move all the furniture up against the walls. In came the barbells, the boxing bags, and all of Sam's other equipment. When Corrie went into the living room the next day to clean, she was flabbergasted at the changes. We heard her deep resonant voice protesting from behind the closed door.

"Sam, put dose possessions of mine in de 'zact, 'dentical spot yo taken dem from. I means dat. I means ev'y word of it. An' don't yo or nobody else ever enter my house agin widout my 'spress commission."

Jenny put up with all this commotion for a month. We had all grown attached to Sam by then. It was like having a gentle, kind giant for a pet. But the idea of his being a boxer was absurd.

Finally, one day Jenny took Sam aside.

"Don't you see what damage you are doing to yourself with all this foolishness?" she asked him. "Arch Persons will never do you any good. Don't break with all those things that mean something to you. Go back to Spring Hill College, to your job and your church."

The next day Sam left on the afternoon bus for Mobile. Jenny had bought him his ticket. It was a sad day for all of us. Just as Sam climbed on the bus, Jenny gave him a big hug and quickly put some money into his pocket before he could protest.

Sam came back many times to visit us in Monroeville, and he was always welcomed. On one trip he brought all us girls silver bracelets with St. Francis medals inside a circle that read "Spring Hill College, Mobile, Alabama" in blue enamel lettering.

Arch had his wildest scheme in the summer of 1930. He discovered a down-and-out Egyptian fellow named Hadjah living with his wife in Meridian, Mississippi. Hadjah knew how to control his breathing by what we call biofeedback today. He could slow his breathing way down and live for a time on very little air.

Arch immediately saw a way to make them all lots of money. He would buy a hearse and a coffin and take Hadjah from small town to small town, burying him in the ground and then digging him up one hour later. It would be sensational, he promised the skeptical Egyptian.

Arch had no trouble talking the starving Hadjah into the scheme. His wife was reluctant, but the family's finances were so bad and the fat wad of cash that Arch waved in their faces so persuasive that she became a convert, too.

Arch brought Hadjah and his family to Monroeville and put them up at the old Vrook Hotel, paying all their expenses. Then he plastered colorful posters all over town. They all said the same thing:

SEE

THE WONDERFUL HADJAH THE GREAT

WORK THE GREATEST MIRACLE OF MODERN TIMES!!!

LIKE LAZARUS OF OLD,

HE WILL BE BURIED DEAD

TO RISE ALIVE FROM THE GRAVE ONE HOUR LATER!!!

Tickets were fifty cents each, children under twelve a dime.

Nothing like this had ever been seen before in Monroeville, and so there was lots of excitement. On the day before the big event a long black hearse with loudspeakers on its roof started to make the rounds of the town. We watched it pull around a corner and slowly move down Main Street toward our house. Truman and Nelle stood on the bone fence, eyes and ears straining. Most of the townspeople stationed themselves along the sidewalks or on their porches, all of them looking in the direction of that hearse.

The hearse kept moving. Double speakers on the top played out a snappy rhythm of guitars, trumpets, and drums. And then a voice began chanting:

> *"In this bier Hadjah lay in sight,*
> *Pronounced as dead as stone.*
> *The coffin lid is clamped on tight,*
> *Poor Hadjah now is gone."*

The hearse drew abreast of our house. Arch's voice boomed forth from the speakers: "See Hadjah the Great, buried and resurrected. The greatest miracle of all times. Saturday afternoon at three o'clock."

Truman started acting like a know-it-all.

"You see, I told you so. That's Hadjah painted on the side, lying in his coffin. That's just before they fasten the lid down.

"That's the most exciting part, just before he is put into the grave and covered up," Truman continued, the other kids listening with drawn breath.

"Who are those people dressed in white, kneeling over the coffin?" Hutch wanted to know.

"Those are the mourners, stupid. They moan and cry and carry on something awful."

"I thought that mourners dressed in black," Hutch insisted.

"Those are professional mourners, dummy," Truman retorted. "They're paid to attend a funeral, and they always dress in white."

We listened to more of the spiel from the hearse.

"With wailing prayers, his soul to save
In death and lifeless sleep.
He's lowered to his earthen grave
And buried six feet deep."

"Do you know Hadjah?" Nelle asked.

"Of course I know Hadjah," Truman answered, and puffed out his chest. "We're good buddies. He's tall and handsome as Rudolph Valentino. He wears a suit of purple velvet with gold buttons and a gold turban on his head. You'd think he was an Egyptian prince from the way he dresses."

In reality, Truman had never seen Hadjah before. His burial clothes consisted of a sheet dyed purple and a towel swirled around his head.

"I know Mrs. Hadjah, too," Truman bragged. "She's beautiful—coal-black hair, black eyes, and mahogany skin. She wears a bright green dress with a red scarf on her head with gold stars all over. She has round gold earrings in her ears as big as the ring in a bull's nose."

Again Truman's imagination had galloped away with him. Poor Mrs. Hadjah's clothes were exceedingly shabby, dirty, and foul-smelling.

The voice continued to boom forth from the hearse as it moved slowly down the street.

"What happens in this lengthy wait,
This everlasting spell?
Does Hadjah enter Heaven's gate?
Or does he visit Hell?"

"How long does he stay buried?" Hutch wanted to know.

"At least an hour, sometimes more," Truman answered confidently. "One time he was down just thirty minutes when Mrs. Hadjah screamed, 'He's dying! Dig him up!' How those gravediggers made the dirt fly. When they got him up, well, he was almost gone, and they had to work like mad to get him back to life."

"I just don't understand how anyone can be buried alive for one full hour and then come back to life," Nelle said.

"You're not supposed to know, silly. He has a secret drug which he takes just before he becomes dead. It stops his heartbeat for a few minutes and his breathing, too. Then he breathes just enough to keep him barely alive. Jenny says one day they're going to dig him up and he really will be dead."

"How come you know so much about him?" another kid asked Truman. "Have you seen it done?"

"I know because my father has handled this act for years. He must have buried him a hundred times all over and everywhere. He's made a lot of money, too.

"I almost saw the funeral last summer," Truman went on, "but just before they buried him, a big movie director from Hollywood showed up and there were no more tickets. So my father gave him mine. I'm going to see it this time, you can bet on that."

The hearse by now had turned the corner and was on the next street over. We could still hear the voice over the loudspeakers:

> "Arise he does and speak aloud,
> As Lazarus did of old.
> The mystery clings like a shroud,
> The answer still untold."

Jenny came out onto the sidewalk, stopped at our gate, gave her umbrella a solid thump, and shouted, "That's the most disgraceful thing I've ever heard. This is sacrilegious. I'm going to the mayor's office and put a stop to this business once and for all."

"Aw, Jenny," Truman protested, "it's just a show like in some movie or the circus when the sword swallower swallows his sword. It's just a trick. I'm going to see it anyway."

"No, Tru, I won't permit that," Jenny replied, and walked

abruptly back into the house. The tone of her voice worried Truman, for he suddenly looked dejected and less confident. When Jenny gave an order in that tone of voice, she always meant business.

The hearse continued its rounds all through the town and nearby countryside announcing the burial for three o'clock on Saturday afternoon.

Truman picked up the song and sang it all over the house except when Jenny was within earshot. Arch arrived back at the house at the end of the day. Truman immediately started working on him, but all he would say was "It's OK with me if it's OK with Jenny."

Truman used every trick he knew, all to no avail. He kicked, stomped, rolled on the floor, and even pretended to go into shock, but Jenny refused to budge. The funeral came off as scheduled on Saturday afternoon. The crowd came from all over the county, and the show was a big success. But Truman was not there.

Arch took the show on the road, playing one small town after another. Each performance was a success. The troupe made money hand over fist. Whenever Arch returned to Monroeville, Jenny and Lillie Mae went to work on him to give up the show. Both thought it was too dangerous, but Arch would beg off, telling them he would do it "just one more time."

Actually, Arch had his private doubts about the show. One day before the funeral he had found Hadjah lying on his bed in a cheap hotel room with a nearly empty bottle of whiskey at his side. Arch was furious.

"Damn you," he told Hadjah, "you shouldn't drink on the day of the burial. You even look like you are drunk."

"You'd get drunk, too, if you were going to be buried at three o'clock this afternoon," Hadjah snapped.

Toward the end of the summer we saw an article on the

front page of the *Mobile Register* with a headline that read "HAD-JAH THE GREAT IS DEAD."

The article gave more details than we wanted to know.

"Yesterday, two thousand sensation-seekers jammed into a small area on Mobile Bay to see what had been billed as 'the greatest miracle of all time.' They paid fifty cents to see Hadjah the Great buried and resurrected.

"What began as an amusing act turned into something more. Hadjah was never brought back to life, despite all the efforts of the local doctors. The actor overplayed his part. The crowd slowly drifted away as the final curtain fell on this great tragedy.

"There will be one more funeral for Hadjah—this, the last one. Admission will be free."

(Truman later put Hadjah's story into his own short story, "A Tree of Night.")

When Arch was not involved in some outrageous scheme or busy at work on the excursion boat, he fretted about Lillie Mae. He had begun to lose her almost from the start of their marriage. Sometimes to improve her spirits he would take her along with him on the the *Capitol,* the fancy riverboat that was his home away from New Orleans. But this only made matters worse. She loved the experience. She was whirled from partner to partner during the dinner dances and was the belle of the party.

Arch told me once about her popularity on board the boat and her complaints afterward about how tedious her life was in New Orleans. "When a beautiful Southern girl from a small town begins to attract that much attention, she is going to start having second thoughts about her marriage," he worried plaintively to me one day.

"Lillie Mae's talking about New York," he continued. "That's all I hear about now—New York, New York, New York.

She wants something else—a richer husband, a career, something more than I can give her."

Arch was right. Lillie Mae was bored and restless. The excitement of the excursion boat waned, and their financial situation failed to improve. Lillie Mae by now had her own car, a secondhand Cadillac, that she used to run back and forth between New Orleans and Monroeville. She never brought Arch with her anymore. She always came alone.

When Arch came to Monroeville for a weekend visit, he and Lillie Mae quarreled constantly.

"Oh, God. This is hopeless. Don't you touch me!" we would hear Lillie Mae say through the closed door of their bedroom.

"What's wrong, Lillie Mae?" Arch would whine. "You always accepted my connubial caresses willingly enough before."

"If I accepted your 'connubial caresses,' as you so quaintly put it, it was out of a sense of obligation and duty. Nothing more. You get one thing straight, Arch Persons. If you want any more of those 'caresses,' then you call on Miss Five Fingers. Because I surely am not about to provide them."

Lillie Mae felt free as a married woman to indulge her passions in a way she never had done when she was a young woman of eighteen. She acted as though she were not married and certainly not the mother of a small child. She always had a circle of admiring men around her.

Corrie told Jenny, "Dat Lillie Mae mus' have a glory hole to beat all dem glory holes. Dat chile acts like no po' white but a low white dat is spawned in de deep hot South."

Lillie Mae had constant fights with Corrie over the way she conducted herself and the provocative style in which she dressed. Corrie especially objected to the full swinging skirts that Lillie Mae liked to wear.

"Lillie Mae," Corrie would complain, "when you wears dem

skirts, it jes' puts it right up in a man's face. Yo gots no shame, woman."

"You shut your mouth, Corrie. You stop picking on me."

Lillie Mae's discontent affected her relations with almost everyone in the house. She called Bud a lazy old pinched-assed man. Callie she hated, referring to her as a peevish alley cat that needed a good jazzing. Sook was no more to her than a common servant. She and Jenny continued to fight like two tigers in a cage.

Lillie Mae took no interest whatsoever in Truman. She hardly noticed him when he was around. One day Truman went back to the kitchen to find Sook. Instead he overheard his mother talking to Little Bit about him.

"I know it is contemptible of me, Little Bit, but I just can't stand the sight of my son—not because he is my child but because he is not my child."

Truman stood outside the doorway and listened.

"That boy is so strange, so utterly strange," she went on. "He does not look or act like a normal boy. He's just like his father sometimes—little Miss Mouse Fart."

Little Bit understood that this was Lillie Mae's pathetic attempt to excuse herself from the responsibility of raising her own child.

Sometimes during the night when he was restless, Truman would leave Sook's side and prowl through the house. He would overhear his parents arguing in their room and then tell us in the morning what they had said.

"Lillie Mae! Please don't leave me," he would hear his father pleading. "I can't go on without you now."

Lillie Mae would withdraw in repulsion at his plea.

"What's the matter with you, Arch?" she would reply. "The idea that you can make this marriage last forever is sheer lunacy. When the time comes to part, we will part."

Truman could actually feel his father and mother alone in their room, eating themselves away with unhappiness and mutual hatred. "Is this what happens when people get married?" he asked us one day. Lillie Mae's visits to Monroeville threw Truman into severe depressions. He would mope about during the days, listless and broken-spirited, until she went back to New Orleans.

As I said earlier, the sight of an attractive, well-dressed man still put goose bumps up and down the inside of Lillie Mae's thighs. She grew bolder and more shameless about satisfying her needs than she had been before her marriage. When Lillie Mae returned to Monroeville, she used me as her ticket to credibility and respectability. Whenever she went out with a man who had taken her fancy, I went along—not as a chaperone (Lillie Mae would have none of that) but as her cover to fool society. By then I was old enough to know my cues and would discreetly disappear whenever Lillie Mae wanted time alone with her boyfriend of the moment.

I remember clearly one afternoon about 1929 when Lillie Mae made a date with a young pharmacist who had just moved into town, Clay Haley. The three of us went out to an old grist mill that stood abandoned at Hatter's Pond outside town, a quiet, private place where lovers could go and not be disturbed. Years before old Mrs. Hatter had walked into the cold, black water of the pond one Sunday morning and drowned. The neighborhood gossip was that this gentle woman could not endure her husband's Saturday night drunks and debaucheries with the black prostitutes in Rooktown.

Clay had a terrible crush on Lillie Mae, who was clearly far more glamorous than any other woman he had known before. Still, he was reluctant to start an affair with a married woman in a small town. The two of them discussed the problem as though I were not even there. I sat a few feet to one side, pretending to watch several birds playing near the old mill.

"Everybody in this town knows you are married," Clay insisted. "My boss has already warned me about taking up with a married woman. In a small town everybody knows everything. Don't you care what people'll say? I certainly do."

"Damn you, Clay," Lillie Mae snapped back, "how can you give two cents for what those people think? Did you ever watch the women in this town in church with their little birdy stares at any attractive man who walks down the aisle? Some of them are as rutty as a sow wanting a boar."

I could tell that Clay was shocked by Lillie Mae's boldness. The two of them sat at the edge of the boards, dangling their feet into the brown waters of the millpond, making quick little patterns in the sandy bottom with their toes.

"If your husband doesn't take care of you and the boy," Clay asked Lillie Mae, "why do you stay with him?"

Lillie Mae glanced sideways at Clay. He had that hangdog look that Arch so often wore, and the last thing she wanted was a lovesick puppy dog trailing behind her. Lillie Mae's affairs of the heart were hardly ever more than affairs for a day.

"Clay, listen to me," she said to him sternly. "I don't want to listen to all this rot. I came to the pond to have a good time and not to be made into a vestal virgin. For two cents I will get into my car and drive home this minute."

"Oh, no, Lillie Mae," Clay said hurriedly. "You stay here, and I won't say anything more about it. Please, I promise."

Lillie Mae didn't say anything more. She turned her back on Clay, reached down into her brassiere, and pulled out her patty-cake makeup. After surveying her face carefully, she made all the necessary repairs.

"Well, Clay," Lillie Mae snapped when she was done, "are we going to sit here on these rotten boards all day, or are we going to have some fun and go skinny-dipping? By the way, you wouldn't have a whet of white lightning with you, would you?

It's getting chilly and if we go in swimming, I don't want to get cramps."

Clay got flustered. "Lillie Mae, I would never carry anything like that with me, not when I am with a lady," he protested. "I would never think of asking a girl—why, did you know . . ."

Before Clay could finish, Lillie Mae shrugged her shoulders haughtily and said, "Sweet Jesus, haven't you learned yet that liquor can sing? When it gets inside you, it turns your blood warm and starts to sing a song. Sometimes it sings a wicked and lustful song. Sometimes it sings a song that gives courage and strength. The thing is, you never know which song it will sing. Well, so much for this afternoon. I am going home."

Lillie Mae abruptly stood up, slipped her shoes back on, and started back disgusted toward the car. Clay jumped up and hurried after her, trailing behind her as they walked through the weeds. He finally caught up with her, screwed up his courage, and put his arm around her waist. The trail had become thick with underbrush and saplings. Bloodroot bloomed everywhere. Clay could tell that Lillie Mae was angry. Whenever she came to a puffball, she kicked it impatiently. We watched the small clouds of mustard-green smoke that erupted each time she stepped on one.

Suddenly Lillie Mae whirled around, her skirt lifting up and exposing her slim brown thighs and calves. Her feet were small and highly arched. She was completely confident.

"I swear, Clay, wouldn't this be the perfect place to take our pleasure?" Lillie Mae said saucily. "Why, every move we'd make would explode a puffball!"

Lillie Mae laughed as she talked. She watched Clay out of the corner of her eye to gauge the impact her words had on him. They stopped and then lay down in the underbrush among the bloodroot and puffballs.

I walked discreetly ahead and sat down in the shadows beneath some trees out of their sight. Dusk was misting down. A chill from the pond was settling on the ground. Shapes were fast losing their distinctiveness in the approaching darkness. The air was sweet and fresh.

Later Lillie Mae and Clay walked up the trail toward me. His hair was dark with sweat and pasted to his forehead. His usually bland voice had an edge to it. One glance at him and I knew Clay was as happy as a hoot owl in a chinaberry tree.

On the way home Lillie Mae suddenly swerved her car off the main road and onto another that led to a large sugarcane mill. During the season when the sugarcane ripened, the mill ground the cane and cooked the syrup seven days a week. During the sugar harvest the mill was a popular gathering spot for the townspeople. The sugar mill worked like a merry-go-round. As the oxen walked slowly around and around, the cane was pushed into the spokes of the grinder, and pure sugarcane juice ran out of a pipe into a big vat. Tin cups hung above the vat, and children, as well as adults, darted between the oxen to snatch a drink of the sweet juice. After the syrup had been boiled, it was as clear as spring water.

Almost too late, Clay realized where Lillie Mae was headed. This would never do! Why, everybody in town would be there, probably even her own little boy.

With a sudden, resolute move, Clay reached over and switched off the ignition. "Turn this car around and go home," he ordered.

Lillie Mae turned to him with scorn and slapped his thigh with a flat, painful blow. But she headed the car back toward town.

On the short ride back into Monroeville, Clay did not say a single word. He was utterly deflated and fully aware that he would never see Lillie Mae again. We dropped Clay off and then drove home.

Little Bit heard Lillie Mae's car stop in the backyard. She

left the kitchen and hurried outside to warn her that Jenny was waiting inside, angry as a trapped hornet. Lillie Mae had always been Little Bit's favorite.

"Lawd Gawd! Miz Lillie Mae, looks lak dere's trouble layin' fer yo. Miz Jenny is gwine roas' yo in hell! Ain't yo heared? Dat sorry Arch Persons is a-coming back tonight from New Orleans!"

Lillie Mae told Little Bit not to worry. We walked through the kitchen. Chicken was frying on the stove. The smell of hot sweet-potato pone filled the air. Off in the distant reaches of the house we could hear Jenny complaining about Lillie Mae. This did not bother her, however, for Lillie Mae always had an ability to shut out those things that she didn't want to hear.

"Where is Lillie Mae, for God's sake?" Jenny was calling to Bud. "Arch Persons will be here soon from New Orleans. What in the name of sweet Jesus does she think she is doing? Riding all over the county in broad daylight with heaven knows who. When Arch leaves here again, he is taking his wife back to New Orleans with him."

Little Bit poked forlornly at the fire in her stove. "Miz Jenny gets mighty upset at dat Lillie Mae struttin' round lak she owns de roost," she said to me. "She's proud of Lillie Mae but she don' want no scandal."

When Jenny saw Lillie Mae, she cut loose with a torrent of abuse.

"What's the matter with you, Lillie Mae?" she demanded. "Don't you know that you can't act this way? We have lived in this town all our lives and are part of the original gentry."

Lillie Mae smiled tolerantly. "Jenny," she said with insincere sweetness, "don't you know the word *gentry* is old-fashioned and not used anymore?"

"Damn you," Jenny screamed. "If you don't like *gentry* how about *whore*? I'll wager you've been out with a bunch of lying, idle, bourbon-drinking, no-good white trash."

Truman sat in a chair near the window and watched the quarrel between Jenny and his mother. Queenie, his dog, lay at his feet. When Lillie Mae walked into the room, he had shrunk back into his chair as still as death.

Lillie Mae refused to argue with Jenny. Instead she rushed over to her son. "Oh, you wonderful, sweet, darling boy," she gushed. "I do love you. You know that, don't you, Truman?" And then just as suddenly she swept out of the room.

Sook got up from her chair and came quickly across the room to where Truman sat. She sat down beside him, took him onto her lap, and held him tightly. A stillness settled over the house, if only temporarily.

Arch knew that Lillie Mae was cheating on him; however, he never had the courage to confront her directly on the matter. But he opened up and talked to me at length about his fears. One day he told me that Hamp and Albert Henderson had warned him years before not to marry Lillie Mae. It was the afternoon on which he made his first date to see her, after they had met on the sidewalk in front of Monroe Drugs. Arch had told them then that he had met the girl he would marry.

"Boy," Hamp warned Arch later that day out at the big Henderson Plantation, "you watch out for that Faulk girl. She swings her hips at everything wearing britches. That gal was born to strut her stuff. Damn! I couldn't sleep at night being married to that sizzler. Why, a man would never have any peace of mind. She would want to be jazzed every hour on the hour. She's just built naturally for the bed. From the day you marry Lillie Mae, it is going to be 'Come on, Hot Pepper. Get hot!' Arch, boy, ain't no way you can handle that. Stick to Rooktown. Fewer problems that way."

"You listen to my brother, Arch," Albert put in. "You don't want no gal that sticks what she's got right up in your face. Why, that Lillie Mae tosses hers around like it was chicken feed in a henhouse. She's only going to be trouble for you."

Arch sat there in his chair on the big veranda of the plantation house, sipping his bourbon and ice. "So, you two Hendersons see things exactly alike about Lillie Mae?" he said in a strained voice.

"We see things exactly alike," answered Hamp. "Arch, you are a fop if you marry that girl."

"Damn it all," Arch shouted, jumping up from his chair. "I am going to marry Lillie Mae. I don't care what you say. You two are jealous, that's all. You lived here all your life and are only just now seeing her. Well, you lost out, see?"

"No, Arch, that's not it at all," Albert said in a more conciliatory tone. "One final piece of advice, and then we drop this subject. If you do marry Lillie Mae, then you crack your whip. And you crack it hard, damn it, man."

Arch paused after telling me of that afternoon almost seven years before.

"They were right, Tiny, they were right," he admitted to himself as much as to me. "You know, Tiny, there are times when I feel like that rabbit and the Tar Baby in the Uncle Remus story. The harder I hit, the stucker I get."

Lillie Mae returned to Monroeville more often after 1926. That was the year she took on Tecumseh Waterford as her lover. He had gone off to Mobile to medical school and been trained as a doctor. Teshu returned to his reservation to work with his people. The two started to meet regularly, sometimes in the woods alongside the river that flowed past the Indian settlement and sometimes in secret places near Monroeville. Lillie Mae often took me along when she thought there might be a danger of her and her lover being seen. Teshu was her great passion, and she gave herself completely to him.

I think Lillie Mae knew that if she divorced Arch and married Teshu, her life would be secure and she would put an end to the turmoil in her heart. She was tempted by the prospect, and God knows, Teshu tried his best to persuade her to do just that. But Lillie Mae could never bring herself to make that final commitment. By 1930 the glitter of New York City proved too strong a temptation. Lillie Mae finally made up her mind. She would leave Arch, go to New York, and start a new life.

Teshu must have sensed that his relationship with Lillie Mae had reached another one of those critical junctures and that he would lose her once again. Years later, after Lillie Mae's suicide, Joe Capote sent us a box of his wife's personal effects, mostly relating to her Monroeville years. Included in a bundle of letters was one from Teshu. The sheets on which it was written had yellowed with age and were broken at the creases where it had been folded and refolded a hundred times. It read as follows:

[no date, no address]

Dear Lillie Mae,

I write you this letter out of an utter despair that is almost suicidal.

I have always been afraid of the day you would marry someone else, and yet I wanted you to because I thought you would be safe, away from the danger of me and the life you would have shared as the wife of an Indian.

My darling, I know you were in love with me and I know that loving me as you did, I might inflict upon you a terrible wrong. [Teshu here refers to the problems she would have had as the white wife of an Indian in the Deep South.]

When you married into the prominent Troy family, I was desperate. I wanted you. I needed you, selfishly for myself. It seemed to me that my only chance for recovery lay in your arms. Loving you, desiring you as passionately as I always have, you would be my only hope.

Lillie Mae, you are so beautiful, so young. Many men will love you throughout your life. Don't cry, my love, don't cry. I realize now that I must go through an endless cycle of hope and despair, each one more abysmal than the last, until I have you again, if only for a short time.

Lillie Mae, you cannot know what it is for me to lie in the arms of a woman whom I love and whose very touch delights and thrills me. Yet I know that your heart is full of falseness, that your lips have lied to me. Yet when you come, I submit.

The letter was signed "T.W."

Lillie Mae went to New York, but when she returned to Monroeville, she always managed to see Teshu. They continued to be lovers right up to the time of her suicide. Teshu never married. He always hoped that someday things would work out, so that he and Lillie Mae would be able to marry.

"I swear, Tiny, that Indian follows me wherever I go. I just can't shut him out of my mind," Lillie Mae confessed to me on one of her visits back to Monroeville from New York. "I close my eyes and remember the fire in his eyes and the passion on his lips. When I move my hands along his neck, I can feel the blood pounding in his veins." I think, too, she enjoyed the sense of danger that accompanied the affair. Joe Capote gave her security and a way into New York society, but he could never give his wife that sense of walking the edge of a precipice, of putting life and limb on the line at each rendezvous.

Lillie Mae told me, too, about her painful final meeting with Teshu before her departure to New York. They met at Martha's Bayou, overlooking the Alabama River. They went to that spot often. There was a small cabin Indian hunters sometimes used, but for the most part the area was secluded, and there was little chance that their activities would be observed.

The two of them stayed together throughout the sunset and into the early hours of the morning. The light from the full moon softened the details of the trees. The deep waters of the river were full of shadows. They made love twice in the darkness of the cabin. Lillie Mae was filled with guilt, for she had planned to break the news to Teshu that in a few days she would board the train to New York City to start a new life.

"Teshu," she finally said, "I have to tell you the truth, no matter what." Their tryst at the edge of the swamp had been sensuous only moments before. The moon suddenly looked weak against the blackness of the night.

"Yes," Teshu said, "you must tell the truth, Lillie Mae."

Lillie Mae held back, fearful of hurting her lover. She sought the words to tell enough, but not too much. The two sat close together, Teshu with his powerful arms embracing Lillie Mae. His very salvation seemed to lie in this contact with her.

"It's almost daylight," Lillie Mae finally said. "I will have to go soon."

Teshu looked down on Lillie Mae in his arms. She saw the beads of sweat on his forehead and high cheekbones. She felt him start to tremble like the leaves of a tree in the wind.

"Don't, Lillie Mae, don't go," Teshu begged her. "I love you. I have never loved anyone but you. Come with me now; come back to the reservation. Be my wife."

"Oh, God, Teshu," she cried. "There's no place we can go. You know that.

"I love you, Teshu," Lillie Mae went on. "You know I do."

There was a long pause. Finally, Lillie Mae broke the silence.

"Teshu, I am divorcing Arch and going to New York to take that modeling course. I can't give this up. I will be back, and I will be just the same with you. But I can't give up New York. It is like you and your medicine and not wanting to practice anyplace but among your people on the reservation. You could not give that up. Please understand."

Teshu took her hands and folded them over the soft swell of her breast and then said simply, "I love you, Lillie Mae, and always will."

While she tried to speak, Teshu turned away and was suddenly gone. It was as if the earth had swallowed him up without a trace.

"It's all over," Lillie Mae spoke aloud. She was numb with pain.

The green world of the wilderness swam about her in the dim twilight of the morning. Lillie Mae started to sob. Her body turned rigid. She ran blindly down the trail back to the spot where she had parked her car. Branches swiped across her face. She hardly felt the stings. Vines caught at her feet. She stumbled and then recovered and hurried on, as though she were pursued by Death.

• CHAPTER NINE •

New York

AUGUST OF 1930 had been a month of pain for young Truman, who would soon be six, and a week of it still remained. The air was hot, humid, and oppressive. Even in the early morning he was depressed at the sight of people he thought mean, tired, and pale, walking as if in a dream. He felt burdened by a sense of loneliness more acute than any he had known in his young life. It was the loneliness of a boyhood without a father, a mother, a brother, or a sister. A constant longing gnawed at him like an empty stomach, but he had only vague impressions of what troubled him.

Truman had a favorite refuge where he retreated in his times of depression, an old icehouse that sat at the edge of Jenny's land beyond Corrie's cabin. The icehouse, which probably dated back to the 1890s, had two large doors, warped with age. Leaning his slight body against one door, Truman could slowly force his way inside to where it was cool and private. He knew that no one would ever disturb him there in the shadows and dampness of his secret hiding place. Portions of the roof had long since collapsed. Shafts of sunlight cut through the darkness, revealing a giant hole in the flooring where blocks of ice had once been hauled up. Seepage from a small spring collected in a shallow pool. Truman liked to sit for hours on end among the ferns with his tiny feet in the cool water, lost in his thoughts and fantasies.

He drifted, dozed—dreaming . . . dreaming.

Truman awoke abruptly. He had slept most of the afternoon. The sunlight had faded. Outside it was starting to get scary dark. Truman knew that he had to get back to the big house. His mother would be off to New York in three days. Jenny was planning a large dinner party on the eve of her departure. He knew what to expect and did not particularly look forward to the occasion.

A heavy embroidered tablecloth would cover the huge dining-room table. Cut-glass water goblets with smaller wineglasses would glitter like ice at each place setting. Truman thought ahead to the guests he knew would be there. A tall lady with bony arms. A grown man with a fluty voice. Women with gaunt shoulders. Uncle Howard with his wet mustache, purple face, and breath that reeked of corn whiskey. Horrid little ladies in their silks with their ever-present lacy black shawls draped precisely over their humped backs, not unlike black buzzards stiffly stepping around.

That Monday Lillie Mae had ordered Truman to go into town with her. He already knew that she would be leaving soon for New York, and he sensed that she probably would not come back to Monroeville except for an occasional visit. The two of them had walked the short distance to the center of the town, exchanging only a few words. As usual, Lillie Mae refused to hold Truman's hand. She always treated him as though he were a neighbor's child, not even family, certainly not her own.

When they reached Fox Henderson's law office, they stopped and went inside. The office smelled of tobacco, dust, whiskey, old leather, and the faint effluvium of generations of mice. Fox Henderson was a thin-nosed and thin-lipped man with cheeks as narrow as a whisper. Long tufts of hair sprouted from his ears. Fox had always thought of Lillie Mae as the most beautiful girl in town. Years before, Lillie Mae had flirted outrageously with him, as indeed she had with many other men in town. But she had only teased him, never fooled around with him, a fact that evidently bothered Fox, who knew her reputation. On occasion he had been known to smack his lips loudly when Lillie Mae walked past his office window. "Damn, there goes one fine piece," he would say. "Now, if I could only get that girl on her back—"

Lillie Mae had hired Fox as her lawyer in the divorce proceedings against Arch. She visited him that day to discuss the final arrangements before her departure for New York and to sign the appropriate papers. There was no reason to drag Truman through the mess, but Lillie Mae had brought him along, probably as a final demonstration of just who wielded the power in her marriage.

Fox knew that whatever Lillie Mae wanted from Arch Persons, he and the judge would see that she received it. That's the way it was then in small Southern towns. You looked after your own. Fox Henderson was from one of the oldest and wealthiest families in Monroe County. He was the head of the local White Citizens Council and had always worked like hell to preserve the white race from the threat of miscegenation.

"Don't you worry none, Lillie Mae," Fox reassured her. "Arch Persons is out of his stomping grounds. Hell, you can get your divorce here without ever stepping into the courthouse. You leave it all to Fox. He'll take good care of you."

Truman thought about that day as he made his way through the backyard toward the house. He saw Sem, the black cook Jenny sometimes hired to assist Little Bit for big parties, sitting in the garden.

Little Bit emerged onto the back porch.

Sem told her that he had to have a place to sleep while preparing the big dinner. He had come in from his cabin on the outskirts of the county a day early to help out.

"Dat cabin of mine is hotter dan a team load of hell," he complained to Little Bit. "I ain't 'bout to walk back dere in de dark, not wid all dem copperheads lyin' 'bout, jist waitin' to bite me dead."

"Damn yo, Sem, don't yo bullshit me none," Little Bit said, all out of patience. "I'se thinks dat de only reason yo come early is so yo can set out an' spy on Lillie Mae an' dat Indian lover she gots fer herself."

"Li'l Bit," Sem said, "youse so mean sometimes dat it's a wonder dat de vines an' de grass don't turn black an' rot where yo walk."

"You's a lazy nigger," Little Bit called to Sem. "Miz Jenny is goin' to put on a big to-do for Lillie Mae an' yo is goin' to do it. So git yore dusty ass up offen dat stump an' git on up to de house."

Truman was quiet that evening at the dinner table, hardly saying a word. He kept his eyes fixed on his mother throughout the meal. Later that evening he retired early to his own bedroom rather than to Sook's room. He did not turn out the light on the small table by his bed.

Truman, still dressed, fell asleep across his big down pillow. That was how Corrie found him the next morning after he failed to get up for breakfast.

Earlier that summer Lillie Mae had seen a notice in the *Mobile Register* of an Elizabeth Arden beauty contest and had entered her picture. She won first prize, which consisted of a trip to New York City and a free beauty course.

When Lillie Mae went to New York, she did not tell Arch that she was going for good. He thought that she was going simply because of the contest and that in a few weeks she would be back in New Orleans. Later Lillie Mae wrote her husband that she would not come back and wanted a divorce.

Arch was crushed, but he did not contest the divorce. "That Lillie Mae is determined to get herself a divorce, and there is not a damn thing I can do about it," he told us. He set about putting his own life in order. Arch continued to visit us in Monroeville, which had become more of a home to him than his parents' place in Troy. But he rarely took more than a passing interest in young Truman.

When Lillie Mae, who was still only twenty-five, stepped off the train in Grand Central Terminal in New York, the first thing she did was to look up a former roommate from her days at Troy State Teachers College, Mary English, a girl from Greenwood, South Carolina. Mary had come to New York to study music. Very much an entrepreneur, she had rented an apartment with a beautiful view of the Hudson River in an old brownstone on Riverside Drive up around the eighties. The apartment had seven bedrooms, all off one long hallway, Pullman style, and a large kitchen. Mary rented out six rooms to working girls for $5 a week with kitchen privileges, $8 if two girls occupied the same room. Mary also taught music on the side.

Lillie Mae moved in with Mary in spite of certain reservations. Life on Riverside Drive was too much like that in a college dormitory for her tastes. She was eager for something much more fashionable. Lillie Mae wrote home to Jenny to say that she doubted she would be there for long. "Besides, I simply cannot understand why a girl like Mary, whose father owns one of the biggest textile mills in the whole state of South Carolina, has to live like she was the daughter of one of his common day laborers," she wrote in obvious disgust over the situation.

Lillie Mae's letters continued to complain bitterly about Mary's old yellow cat that was forever shedding balls of hair and the crowded kitchen with its enameled gas stove, large humpbacked refrigerator, and white enameled table with red stripes around the sides.

Lillie Mae had little choice in the matter, however. Jenny had informed her that she would support her until she found proper employment but that she would have to be economical about it. As Jenny put it, "I've worked my tailbone raw trying to make it, and by damn, you can do the same."

Most of the other girls were in a similar predicament, sometimes much worse. After all, this was 1930, and the country was sliding rapidly into the worst depression of the century. For most of the girls just getting enough food was a daily struggle. Lillie Mae surveyed the scene and quickly saw what had to be done if they were all going to survive. She explained to them that in order for them to eat well, each had to do her part.

"Rule number one, girls: never bring a man back to the apartment for dinner. Make him take you to dinner, and then order a doggy bag and stuff in everything you can—rolls, pats of butter, scraps of meat—anything."

"But we don't have a dog," one of the girls ventured to complain.

Lillie Mae fixed a cold bead on the girl. "Honey, you are off the farm now and in the big city. Try and act the part."

"I know," the girl continued, "but my boyfriend is from Alabama. He is working to save money. We can't afford a restaurant. He buys his food at the A & P, and we cook it here."

"OK, dummy," Lillie Mae ordered, "just get him to buy extra food for the rest of us. You can't expect us to bring food back here for you if you don't do your part for us, do you?"

Mary was horrified at Lillie Mae's calculated approach to life and men. Even to this day when she and I get together (for we have been good friends through the intervening decades), she can't talk about New York or her years in music school without telling at least one story about Lillie Mae.

Poor Mary. She was a pretty girl—tall with fiery red hair and freckles all over her face. But life had not been easy on her. She had been widowed young. Shortly after she married, her husband fell out of a pecan tree and broke his neck. In New York she soon learned that keeping lodgers and giving piano lessons would not pay all her bills. So she got a job as hostess at MacDougal's Alley Restaurant on 8th Street in Greenwich Village.

Lillie Mae was also in for some major disappointments. The first prize in the Elizabeth Arden beauty contest did not open the doors she had hoped; in fact, it proved more of a liability than an asset. (Too many first-prize winners had been brought in from all parts of the country. They glutted the market and were the butt of a great many jokes.) So Lillie Mae looked around for a job. Mary got her one at MacDougal's Alley. Within three months Lillie Mae had been promoted to hostess, and Mary was out.

"My God," Mary complained bitterly to Lillie Mae back in their apartment. "How could you do such a treacherous thing as steal my job? After all I have done for you, too."

"Mary, I am sorry about that, I really am," Lillie Mae said. "But they offered me the job, and I couldn't turn it down. And besides—you had no more chance of holding that job than a whale has of swimming in a frog pond."

"But, Lillie Mae, you asked for my job!"

"Mary, get control of yourself. Really. I sometimes don't know what's become of you. Running a cheap boardinghouse like this. Haven't you any pride? It simply is not a proper place for me to live. I for one am moving out."

"You bet your round rump you're moving out, Lillie Mae," Mary hollered.

"Don't worry about me, Mary. I can get any man I want," Lillie Mae bragged shamelessly. "In no time at all I will be set up in a big, expensive apartment. Just you wait and see."

"I just don't believe you, Lillie Mae," Mary said, almost ready to cry. "You are not only immoral. You are without any true feeling for anybody. You are out for Lillie Mae only. God, but I pity you. Someday you will learn that all that selfishness has only made you the unhappiest person in the world."

By then Mary was beyond being shocked at the things

Lillie Mae did. A few weeks before, she learned that her friend was seeing a Catholic priest.

"My God, Tiny, I simply couldn't believe it at the time," Mary recalled recently. "Lillie Mae even brought him back to the apartment. She told us all that it was strictly spiritual. 'All those candles flickering and the clouds of incense make me feel holy'—those were her exact words. One day Lillie Mae dragged me off to his church for a communion service. My God, I couldn't believe it. Here she was, accepting communion from a priest she wanted to take on as her lover. After the sermon Lillie Mae had the gall to go up to the altar. And when she knelt at the railing, she strained every muscle in her body, so that her breasts looked as though they were ready to pop right out of her blouse. Lillie Mae admitted to me that he never did become her lover, but it certainly was not for any lack of trying on her part! That woman knew no bounds to her behavior."

Well, Lillie Mae did not move out of Mary's apartment just then. Rather the next day she brought home a present for Mary—a little Swiss music box in a mahogany case with a rosewood inlay on the top. It was lovely and played Brahms's *Lullaby*. When she gave it to Mary, she told her how sorry she was for taking her job and hoped she would forgive her. Then she gave Mary a hug and a kiss and presented her with the gift. Mary broke down in tears. Lillie Mae knew her friend all right.

Lillie Mae next landed a better job as the manager of the Green Line Restaurant on Warren Street near Wall Street. It was a very busy place. The restaurant's specialty was Southern cooking. It was famous for its chicken pot pie, fresh strawberry pie, hot sourdough rolls, and three small pots of fresh fruit preserves on each table. The restaurant was in the basement of the building, and you had to walk down a long flight of stairs to reach the dining area. The Green Line's clientele generally had lots of money.

Lillie Mae then persuaded Mary to give up their Riverside

Drive apartment and move with her to the Barbizon-Plaza Hotel. It was a much nicer building with a more fashionable address.

"I don't want these Yankees to think we are poor Southern white trash," she told Mary.

Within a few months of starting work at the Green Line, Lillie Mae had met and infatuated Joe Capote, who had passed himself off as a Cuban millionaire. Actually, he was a controller at Taylor, Pinkham & Company, located a short walk from her restaurant on Worth Street in the textile district. Joe was from Havana, Cuba; however, he did not have any million dollars in his bank account. But he made a fair amount of money, spent it as though he had a great deal more, and moved in a fast, stylish circle of socially prominent people.

Lillie Mae sized up Joe the first time he came into her restaurant and told a waitress nearby, "Now that's my kind of man. You watch. I'm going to marry him." She did, too. I always had to hand it to Lillie Mae. She was damn good at getting what she wanted.

In the meantime Mary had landed a job with an airline. It looked as though the two girls from small Southern towns were on their way to success in the big city. Lillie Mae ran a check on Joe Capote and quickly put together a rather complete dossier on the man. She learned he had been born and bred in Havana and that his father had made a fortune running the family's sugarcane plantation. The Capote family was prominent in Cuban political circles. Joe had been in the United States for ten years and had graduated from the Pace Institute in accounting. Later he became a C.P.A. The more Lillie Mae learned about Joe Capote, the better she liked him.

All this had happened in less than a year after Lillie Mae moved to New York. Truman was still in Monroeville. It was as though her marriage and her son had never happened. Occasionally she sent Truman a package of candy from Schrafft's in

New York, usually a big red-and-white swirled lollipop. Her attorney, Fox Henderson, had put through the divorce without any difficulty.

Eventually Joe Capote set Lillie Mae up in an apartment at 425 Riverside Drive at 87th Street. The next thing I knew she wanted me to leave Monroeville for New York and to bring Truman along. This was in the late summer of 1931.

Jenny tried to argue me out of the trip. I had been working days in her store, filling in for Callie, who was sick. Sook was just turning sixty. When Lillie Mae's letter arrived, she was devastated by the prospect of losing Truman. This was the only time I ever saw her beg Jenny for something. Sook wanted her to refuse to send Truman to his mother.

"For God's sake, Sook," Jenny told her, "let that child go. You must know that he has got to be with his mother, if that is what she wants."

"No, no, no!" Sook pleaded hysterically. "His mama and daddy don't give a fig for him. They don't love him. Every time I think of the dreadful way that Lillie Mae has treated him, why, I could poke out her eyes with a red-hot poker. I really could."

Poor Sook. She was frantic. She was losing her life, her reason for existing. When Jenny declined to interfere, Sook rang up Dr. Fripp and tried to get him to deliver some arsenic rat poison. But she was so clearly distraught that he refused to comply and notified Jenny instead. Jenny, in turn, called the family's physician, who gave Sook a sedative.

After Sook had quieted down, Jenny had a long talk with her in her bedroom, trying to convince her that Truman's departure for New York would not mean the end of her world.

"Nanny, Tru is going to New York, but he'll come back to visit us, I promise you that," Jenny said, reassuringly. "Now I want you to pack him a nice lunch to eat on the train. Put in everything he likes—baked chicken with hot pepper sauce, ham biscuits, some of your homemade cucumber pickles, some cubes of cheese . . ."

"And lemon meringue pie, too, Jenny. Don't forget his favorite."

"No, Nanny, make some fresh lemon tarts instead of the lemon meringe pie. That won't keep, and the meringue will slip off. And give him a bag of boiled peanuts and some shelled Stuart pecans. Anything else?"

"Yes, grapes and persimmons, if I can find them."

"OK, grapes and persimmons."

"When . . . is my darling Tru going?" Sook was too choked up to say more.

"As soon as possible. I'll be driving Tiny and Tru to Flomaton to catch the train. Don't you want to come, too, to see them off?"

"No."

"Don't worry, Nanny, you've given that boy enough love these past seven years to last him a lifetime. He'll write you. And he will be back often to visit you."

"Oh, Jenny," Sook wailed, "I just want to die. They never will let him come back to me. It will never be the same. Please, Jenny, let me die." She broke down again and started sobbing uncontrollably. Jenny called the doctor, who came around again and gave Sook another shot to quiet her nerves.

Truman and I left Monroeville for New York in the early part of September 1931. Lillie Mae and Joe Capote met us at Pennsylvania Station. I still remember clearly what she was wearing that day—a wool suit in navy blue with a red belt, a perky hat with a blue veil, and a white blouse heavily embroidered with sprays of flowers. The outfit was expensive and stylish. Lillie Mae looked even more beautiful than I had remembered her.

I asked her where she had bought her outfit.

"Bergdorf Goodman, dummy," was her reply.

I was a dummy all right, for Bergdorf Goodman at the time meant nothing to me. But I did know right away without being told that Joe Capote had bought it for her.

I then looked more closely at Joe. Lillie Mae had already advised me in her letter that they would be getting married shortly. He was a short man with a small build and a dark, sad face. His hair was black and very fine and thin, like a baby's. The one feature that struck me at our first meeting was his pince-nez eyeglasses. He constantly took them off and put them back on again, and you could always see two small scarlet circles on each side of his nose where the little springs pinched his skin. His glasses gave him an elegant look. There was more politeness than warmth to his greeting of the two of us.

Joe put us all in a taxi, and soon we were at 425 Riverside Drive. They had a large apartment, expensively furnished, facing the Hudson River. There was even a maid's quarters in the rear. The living room was enormous with cobalt-blue carpeting so thick that you sank to your ankles in it as you walked across. There was a fireplace with a mirror above that rose to the ceiling and bookcases on either side, full of expensive, hand-tooled leather-bound volumes. The glass coffee table had gold leaf and silver applied from the back and looked like a crown jewel. Everything in their apartment was first-class. Lillie Mae took me on a tour, pointing out each item, telling me where she had bought it and how much it had cost.

Truman and I shared a bedroom in the rear. Lillie Mae had the front bedroom with a view of the Hudson River. Joe did not actually live in the apartment. He kept his clothes and his residence at another address. But he spent most of his nights with us. Three or four evenings of every week he called for Lillie Mae to take her out to dinner or the theater. He rarely invited Truman or me along. As the weeks passed, he became more and more casual in his dress around the two of us. It wasn't long before Joe started showing up at the breakfast table in a smoking jacket and pajamas. I knew he was paying the rent and all of Lillie Mae's bills.

I returned to Monroeville in late fall and more or less took over the management of Jenny's store. Callie was slowly dying of cancer and could no longer help her out. Jenny knew that I wanted very much to return to New York and did everything possible to discourage me. She even offered to transfer owner-ship of the store to me if I stayed with them there in Monroe-ville. Jenny was only fifty-eight at the time, and I knew that whatever legal arrangements she made would take effect only at her death. I remained in Alabama until 1932 and then returned to New York at Lillie Mae's urging.

But Lillie Mae was less interested in having a sister nearby than she was in having a live-in baby-sitter for Truman. Joe got me a job with his office of Taylor, Pinkham & Company, a large textile converting firm. I always felt that he offered me the posi-tion because he wanted to be certain that Truman would have proper care and that he and Lillie Mae would be free to live their own lives without being tied down.

I had no credentials whatsoever for office work, but that made no difference to Joe. He installed me as an accounting assistant at a salary of $25 a week, a huge sum to me in those days. My experience in Jenny's store had taught me a great deal about selling and how to deal with the public, but not much else. I suddenly had to confront the fact that I was poorly pre-pared for a career. So I enrolled in night school at New York University, starting with a course in accounting. I hated that. Soon afterward I dropped the accounting and entered the New York School of Culinary Arts to study food preparation, deco-rating, ice sculpture, and management. Later this became one of my most successful careers and one that I dearly loved.

I continued to work for Taylor, Pinkham & Company for the first few months after coming to New York. I received the shock of my life soon after I started when I learned from several of the office girls with whom I had become friendly that the "Miss Burkett," the secretary to the credit manager, was actually Joe Capote's wife! I could not believe my ears. Miss Burkett was a big woman, with short-cropped hair. She spoke in a sharp, crisp voice. She was also quite a bit older than Joe. I could not imagine anyone more of an opposite to Lillie Mae than her.

"My God, why would a dapper man like Joe Capote marry Miss Burkett?" I asked one of the office girls.

I couldn't wait to get back to the apartment. I knew that Lillie Mae had no idea that her man was already married. When I walked into the apartment, Lillie Mae was in her bedroom getting herself ready to go out for dinner with Joe. I sat down on the edge of her bed.

"Lillie Mae, I just found out something about Joe Capote that I think you should know," I said after a moment's hesitation.

"Pray tell, what?" Lillie Mae asked, rubbing some rouge on her cheeks.

"I learned today at work that he is married to a woman by the name of Miss Burkett who works in his office as the secretary to the credit manager."

"Oh, shit," Lillie Mae said. That was one of the rare times I ever heard her say the word. "That son of a bitch. Why didn't he tell me?" She started moaning, like a person who has suddenly been hit a hard blow to the stomach.

"Lillie Mae," I said, "don't you start acting like a fool. Simply tell Joe Capote where to go. You don't need another man with shady ways."

"Tiny," Lillie Mae said after a moment, the tears streaking her face, "don't *you* be a damn fool. What in the name of sweet Jesus would I do if I dropped Joe? I am in a mess. I don't have a job anymore. I've got Truman on my hands now. I couldn't keep this apartment. What the hell can I do?"

"I'll tell you what you can do."

"What?"

"Let's pack our clothes, leave the key to the apartment with the superintendent, and go home to Monroeville. We have enough money between us to buy three train tickets. There's no use dragging out the agony anymore. Let's go!"

"No, I just can't walk out like that. When Joe comes tonight, I'll ask him straight out what is going on."

And that's exactly what Lillie Mae did. She met him at the door, and as soon as she got him in the living room, she popped her question.

"Joe, I am asking you straight—are you married to a woman in your office?"

Joe was startled, caught off guard, but he quickly recovered.

"Yes, that's true. But it's only an arrangement."

"Do you mean you have not lived together as husband and wife?"

"Not for a moment," Joe answered. "I swear it, honey."

I was listening from the hallway. I didn't let on, but I felt that he was lying. His story was too pat. As Corrie would have said, "Gal, dat jist don't wash."

I heard Lillie Mae say again, "No, sir, I just don't believe you. I know you too well, Joe Capote. You simply could not live with a woman without getting something going. Damn, you would bore a hole through the wall to get at her."

"My darling Nina," he said (Nina was his pet name for her; he never called her Lillie Mae), "you just don't understand."

By this time Lillie Mae was getting more and more worked up.

"What do you take me for, Joe Capote? A goose? No damn spic is going to pull the wool over this Southern gal's eyes."

I don't know what happened after that. The two of them went out for dinner. Lillie Mae returned alone about 3:00 A.M.

Well, of course, the whole ugly mess was out now. Lillie Mae had to decide what to do. I knew that she would never return to Monroeville. That would have been an admission of failure and played straight into Jenny's hands. I also knew that she would eventually marry Joe. He represented her ticket to wealth and social position.

Joe was moonstruck and determined to win Lillie Mae back. He showered her with gifts—flowers, perfume, jewelry. They dined out every evening at some very expensive restaurants. They partied at the Latin Quarter, where Joe loved to dance the rumba to the band of Xavier Cugat. Soon Joe was back again, spending his nights at 425 Riverside Drive.

"Damn it, Lillie Mae," I asked her one day, "what the hell is going on between you and Joe? Has he agreed to get a divorce and marry you?"

"None of your damn business, Tiny," Lillie Mae snapped back.

She was bitter toward me because I had found out. We had angry words on the subject.

"Is this what you brought your son to New York to see?" I demanded.

No answer from Lillie Mae.

"Why should Joe buy the cow?" I asked her. "Hell, he gets the milk for free."

Soon afterward I quit my job at Taylor, Pinkham. When I returned to the apartment, I went into Lillie Mae's bedroom to tell her the news and also my intention to move out. She was sitting on the edge of her bed, pulling on her silk stockings.

"Lillie Mae, I am leaving," I announced. "As soon as I can get an apartment, I will come back for my clothes."

Lillie Mae didn't even look up at me. She just kept pulling on her stockings. I knew she was hurting inside. I was, too, but I still had another problem to deal with—Truman.

I went back to his room. There was no need for words. Truman knew. How he knew I do not know.

I returned to Monroeville for six months. Lillie Mae hired a woman to take care of Truman. She called me constantly to beg me to come back to New York. She told me that Joe had filed for a divorce and that she was getting instruction in the Catholic church. As soon as his divorce became final, they got married. No one from the family was present. Lillie Mae told me later that they did not get married in the Catholic church because both of them were divorced. She also learned that Joe had been married yet another time, back in Cuba. Their marriage took place in late 1933. Afterward Joe legally adopted Truman as his son, at Lillie Mae's urging.

When I returned to New York, Lillie Mae had a job as manager of the Stirling Bakers on 39th Street and Ninth Avenue. She had met Mrs. Stirling while buying for the Green Line Restaurant. Stirling Bakers furnished pies and cakes to the better accounts in the area. I took up residence once again at 425 Riverside Drive. Lillie Mae secured for me a job as night manager at Stirling. I had to go in at three o'clock in the morning, make out the order for the day, see that the trucks were loaded, and then visit the produce and vegetable market on Washington Street to buy all the fresh fruit for the day's pies.

Mrs. Stirling went to Europe for an extended holiday. Before she left, she asked me to house-sit her apartment on 39th Street on the East River. That suited me just fine. I had no rent or other expenses in regard to the apartment and felt like a queen. The place had been beautifully decorated by W. & J. Sloane. Three months later Mrs. Stirling returned and took over my duties as night manager.

I took an apartment on West 9th Street in an old brownstone between Fifth and Sixth avenues. I also managed to get a position with a large institutional food company, serving colleges. After I moved into my own apartment, I always knew that I could count on finding Truman on my doorstep late every Friday afternoon when I returned from work. He usually spent his weekends with me.

I lived on the third floor. As we climbed the stairs together, Truman always had some sort of tale to tell me. He was fascinated by words and played at being a writer, even then. His mother had given him an old typewriter, and he spent hours alone in his room, pecking away. I think part of it was an escape from his domestic situation.

"Did I ever tell you, Tiny, about the time I tried to write my first story?" Of course he had. But I let him go on. "Well, I lay in that bed all night and thought and thought about how I would start it off. I just couldn't start it. But then another time I just sat down, and it all came out so fast I couldn't type fast enough to keep up."

Truman had told me at least a dozen versions of what had happened when he tried to write his first story. Sometimes he brought along copies of his stories and let me read them. They were much better than you would have thought, given his eleven years. His perception was acute, even then.

Truman loved New York. To him as a child in Monroeville, New York had represented adventure, excitement, glamour, and, of course, a family life with his mother. He thought that because his mother had requested him that things would be different in the future, that she would be the loving, caring mother he had always wanted and never had. But the reality proved very different from his childish fantasies. At first Lillie Mae worked seriously at her responsibilities of being a mother, but she soon lost interest. And the elfin Truman—small, thin, and "pretty"—hardly satisfied her requirements of what a "real son" ought to look like. She spent less and less time with him, relegating his care to me and then later to a live-in governess/maid. Lillie Mae and Joe changed apartments every eighteen months or so, and Truman had little opportunity to make friends his own age. She shifted him from school to school, as his grades deteriorated, hoping to find one that would "take charge" and "make a man" out of Truman. For a time he attended a Jesuit school on the West Side of Manhattan. Truman flunked out there. Lillie Mae eventually enrolled him in St. John's Military Academy, which, of course, Truman hated.

After an initial period of euphoria, Truman was a depressed, alienated, and lonely child for much of his time in New York. Lillie Mae and Joe traveled often, especially to Cuba in the summers, but they rarely took Truman along, preferring to send him back to Monroeville for those months when he was on vacation from school. For several years, as Truman developed into adolescence, I think I was probably his only friend and confidante in New York City. As I said, he spent most weekends with me in my small Greenwich Village apartment. We were great friends and shared many little adventures about the city.

Truman's great escape at this time was the movies, which he loved with a passion. He frequently cut school and rode the bus to 42nd Street to spend the afternoon sitting in the dark watching the flickering images on the screen. He was most particular about this. Truman never saw movies in the neighborhood theaters. He insisted upon coming into town to the vicinity of 42nd Street and Broadway. Our Friday nights together were always movie nights.

Truman's Friday night movie binges had a certain rhythm to them. First, he would pick out a good double feature. He loved the Rockettes, so sometimes it was Radio City Music Hall. We generally got in about eight o'clock. This would put us out about midnight. Then we had doughnuts and coffee at the Mayflower Do-nut snack bar. (Truman had picked up a coffee habit back in Monroeville.) Then about one o'clock we took in a horror film. Young Truman had extraordinary endurance.

He never seemed to need sleep, at least not when he had the opportunity to see a movie.

I remember one Friday evening—actually early Saturday morning—when I was simply too exhausted to take Truman to his usual horror film.

"Truman," I implored him, "it's too late for another movie. I'll never sit through it. Let's call it quits for the night."

"No," Truman shouted. "I want my horror film."

A new Boris Karloff film had opened at the Paramount, and Truman was dying to see it. We were in front of the theater, and he looked longingly at the scary posters.

"I suppose you think you are going in there, do you, young man?" I asked. "Well, you are not. I am taking you home with me. I need some sleep."

Truman didn't say another word. Instead he fell over backward and landed on the sidewalk with a leaden thump. He began to twist and moan, as though he were having an epileptic fit.

A crowd quickly gathered.

"Call the police," one man hollered. "That kid looks like he is in bad shape."

I was humiliated and embarrassed. I grabbed Truman's hand, dragged him upright, and marched him to the box office.

"OK, you win," I told him.

We hurried inside the theater.

"Let's get a good seat down front before they are all gone," Truman said, racing ahead.

Truman has always had bad eyesight, a trait he inherited from his father. As a child, when he went to the movies, he loved to sit in the exact middle of the fourth row. For me it was uncomfortable. For Truman it was just perfect.

On Saturday we ate out at a restaurant. The gaudier and more garishly furnished the restaurant, the more popular it was with Truman. He loved Gage & Tollner's in Brooklyn and

White's down on Fulton Street. He shunned places like the Automat. Truman would tell me with a great deal of contempt that people who ate at the Automat were just "too ordinary for words."

On those weekends when I felt broke, we would eat at the White Tower on 8th Street with its glaring white tile and day-old chicken pot pies for half price. Or at Stewart's Cafeteria on Sheridan Square in the Village, a favorite with down-and-out artists, novelists, and poets. Truman liked to go there and people-watch.

Truman also loved the streetcars that jostled through the New York traffic. He begged me one day to ride on a streetcar rather than take a bus.

"Truman," I asked him, "what in the world is so fantastic about riding in a noisy old streetcar?"

"Oh, Tiny," he told me, "that's their charm. They are saying, 'Here I come, get out of my way.' And that's how I want to be, silly."

Another favorite of Truman was the New York Museum of Natural History. The grizzly bear, Florida panther, and *Tyrannosaurus rex* exhibits all fascinated him, especially the latter. He loved its name and rolled it around on his tongue. It was a word we all got sick of hearing. Truman has always loved long and complicated words.

We both hated the New York subway, but when our finances were low, we had no choice. I was always bewildered by the maze of underground trains. Truman disliked the dank odor of many of the cars. But when we visited the Battery, usually on Sunday mornings, we had to take the subway. Truman loved the aquarium there with its glass tanks full of brilliantly colored fish that flashed and darted in front of his eyes.

Sometimes when Truman had a new experience, he would remember Sook, whose entire life had been spent in Monroeville. The cormorants at the aquarium fascinated him.

"I'm going to write home to Sook about them," he told me one day. "You know she has never seen a movie, and I just know that she has never been to an aquarium. I wish I had a picture of a cormorant to send her."

"Don't worry about that, Truman," I advised him. "When you write and describe the cormorants, she will see them in her mind's eye as clearly as if she had been here with you."

I waited a moment, and then I asked him another question.

"Truman, do you miss Sook and things in Monroeville? Don't you want to go back there?"

"Yes, Tiny, I do miss Sook, Nelle, Corrie, and all of Little Bit's good things to eat. But I love New York, too, and all the new things to do. Everything here is so grand. I love it here and I am never, never, ever going to leave, except to visit Monroeville in the summer."

"I am glad you like it, Truman. I don't."

"Why, Tiny?"

"I can't get use to seeing a beautiful red geranium growing out of a tin can. And the flowers here have no smell. Even the trees seem to fall to pieces like they were made of ashes."

Truman thought a moment.

"I know, Tiny," he finally said. "But just think of all the beautiful things to do and see here."

"Well, Truman, a child shouldn't spend his precious childhood among strangers. He should be where he is loved and around things that are familiar."

I became friendly again with Lillie Mae and Joe after they married; they often invited me to join them for dinner at one of their favorite restaurants. Joe tried in his way to be a father of sorts to Truman. He gave his adopted son every advantage that money could buy. (But I never knew whether he sent Truman to St. John's Military Academy as a way of furthering his education or simply as a handy means of getting him out from underfoot around home.)

One time Joe asked Truman, then thirteen, if there wasn't anything special that he wanted.

"Yes, I would like a dog," Truman answered promptly.

"Fine, I'll buy you one. But why didn't you tell me before?"

"Why should I tell you?" Truman answered coldly. "I don't belong to you. I don't even like you."

"I'm sorry you don't like me, Truman, but I will buy you a dog anyway. How's that?"

"Well, I should like a bulldog. You know—the kind that will bite a body's head off."

(Joe never did buy Truman that bulldog, but years later Humphrey Bogart gave him just such a dog. Truman named it Bunky. On July 15, 1961, Truman wrote me from Palermo, Sicily, that Bunky had died and enclosed a picture of a new dog named Charley.)

Lillie Mae entertained constantly, throwing big parties attended by lots of socially prominent people. She had always been a social climber and was now in her element. Truman would wander among the crowds of guests, dressed in his linen suit, preening like a peacock and holding a frosted glass in his hand.

"That's my mother," he would tell a group of strangers, pointing out Lillie Mae, who swished her way through the crowds, oblivious of her son.

But underneath Truman was scared and uncertain. He felt like the shipwrecked sailor who tries desperately to catch hold of a slippery rock to save himself from the storm's waves. He was changing, becoming different from other boys his own age. He didn't understand what was happening and had no one to turn to but me.

Lillie Mae continually attacked him for behavior she thought effeminate and improper. She rode him constantly.

"Truman, I swear, we give you every advantage, and still you can't behave. If it were just the failing out of school, I could take it. But, my God, why can't you be more like a normal boy your age? I mean—well, the whole thing about you is so obvious. I mean—you know what I mean. Don't take me for a fool."

One time Lillie Mae asked Truman point-blank about his friendship with a boy from Macon, Georgia. He noticed that all the time she was interrogating him, his mother was not looking directly at him, but rather surveying her own figure and dress in the full-length mirror on his bedroom door. Truman tried to find some sharp retort to his mother's persistent questioning, but none came. He was tongue-tied and embarrassed. Finally, he simply gave up, turned away, and walked out of the room, choking back his tears.

These were tough years for Truman. It was hard for him to realize what was happening to him, and with no compassion from his mother he traveled a lonely road. I will have to say this for Joe Capote—I never once heard him make any complaint about Truman's behavior.

Joe and Lillie Mae moved to Greenwich, Connecticut, in 1937, and I remained in New York City. I saw far less of Truman during that time. He came to the city as often as possible, but his mother was reluctant to let him travel by himself.

I met Jim Rudisill, the man who was to become my husband. A boy from Macon, Georgia, whom I had been dating, introduced us. Jimmy worked for a large textile company in Manhattan. We married in 1938 and soon afterward moved to Augusta, Georgia.

Truman walked down a path that took him farther and farther from Monroeville. As the years passed, his links with his Southern past grew weaker and weaker. As I look back on those later years, I sense that Truman had a need to cut himself off deliberately from the people and places that gave his childhood meaning and substance to much of his early fiction.

Today, forty-five years later, the break is complete. Truman has turned away from his Southern background, denying all of us who had shared those years with him. One by one he cut us off—his father, Jenny, Nelle, finally me. For fifteen years now he has refused to take my phone calls. My letters are returned unopened. When Truman travels through the South today, he no longer comes to visit.

But I prefer to remember the happy times together—the picnics at Hatter's Mill, the big Christmas dinners, Sook's medicine making, the snug warmth of Corrie's cabin, the smells of Little Bit's kitchen, Bud and Sylvester in their cotton field shortly before harvest time, and the endless stream of Tom Sawyerish adventures about Monroeville.

Shortly before Jimmy and I left New York for Georgia in 1938, I took Truman shopping in Bloomingdale's for one last gift. I let him pick out two Aynsley china cups and saucers decorated with huge yellow hand-painted roses. They were a bit gaudy but beautiful in their way. Truman said then that he liked them because they reminded him of the yellow rosebushes in Jenny's yard.

Perhaps someday Truman will walk past another yellow rosebush and remember Monroeville. Off in a distant corner of his mind he will hear Corrie's voice coming to him through the mists of the past—

"Chile, don't yo eber fergit dat it ain't death you'se got to fear de most. It's livin' widout love."

Index